MW01166360

THA**ı** ɪᴠⅼ ᴡ ᴡᴏʀʟᴅ

– ★ –

The

SELECTED POEMS

of

SARAH PIATT

(1861-1911)

* _ *

Larry R. Michaels

Mac-A-Cheek Foundation for the Humanities
Piatt Castles, West Liberty, Ohio
* *
Bihl House Publishing
Toledo, Ohio
1999

The editor gratefully acknowledges the early encouragement given by Paula Bennett as to the worth of preserving Sarah Piatt's poetry, and to the further encouragement along the way by Sally Gray of the Louisville Public Library, Heidi Yeager at the Canaday Center of The University of Toledo, Jim Nash formerly at the Piatt Castles, Barbara Lyons of The Ohio State University Press, and by Margaret Piatt and Angie Warye of the Mac-A-Cheek Foundation for the Humanities based at the Piatt Castles in West Liberty, Ohio.

The Mac-A-Cheek Foundation for the Humanities, created in partnership with the Piatt Castles, Inc., is a not-for-profit organization formed to promote scholarship in research to better understand the life, culture, and environment relating to the heritage of the Mac-A-Cheek region in Central Ohio. An archive of Piatt papers is being made available to scholars at the Piatt Castles in West Liberty, Ohio.

Published August 11, 1999, in cooperation with the Mac-A-Cheek Foundation for the Humanities. Printed in the United States of America. All rights reserved.

FIRST EDITION

For ordering information contact the Mac-A-Cheek Foundation for the Humanities, P. O. Box 166, West Liberty, OH 43357, or Bihl House Publishing, 548 Robindale Ave., Oregon, OH 43616.

ISBN 1-883829-07-0

CONTENTS

Introduction 9

Piatt's Dedication 36

From The Nests at Washington (1864):

My Ghost 37
Gaslight and Starlight 39
My Wedding Ring 41
To Marian Asleep 42
Hearing the Battle 44

From A Woman's Poems (1871):

The Fancy Ball 45
After Wings 46
My Babes in the Wood 47
Shapes of a Soul 49
Death before Death 50
Offers for the Child 52
Earth in Heaven 54
Her Last Gift 55
A Child's First Sight of Snow 56
Questions of the Hour 57
Talk about Ghosts 59
Playing Beggars 61
A President at Home 63
An After-Poem 64
Army of Occupation 65

From A Voyage to the Fortunate Isles (1874):

There Was a Rose 66
If I Were a Queen 67
Their Two Fortunes 71

The Order for Her Portrait 72
"I Want It Yesterday" 73
Marble or Dust? 74
Sweetness of Bitterness 76
Beatrice Cenci 78
Over in Kentucky 79
Say the Sweet Words 81
Leaving Love 82
The Black Princess 84
The Funeral of a Doll 86
Crying for the Moon 88
Aunt Annie 89
The Palace-Burner 91
"I Wish that I Could Go" 93
This World 95
A Masked Ball 97
A Woman's Birthday 99

From <u>That New World</u> (1877):

That New World 100
The Altar at Athens 101
Lady Franklin 102
Her Cross and Mine 103
Counting the Graves 104
We Two 105
Sad Wisdom--Four Years Old 106
No Help 107
Asking for Tears 108
Calling the Dead 109
Tradition of Conquest 110
A Dead Man's Friends 111
Peace Making 112
The Little Boy I Dreamed About 113
The Baby's Hand 115
"More about Fairies" 116
The Sad Story of a Little Girl 118

From <u>Dramatic Persons and Moods</u> (1880):

Reproof to a Rose 120
A Pique at Parting 121
The Descent of the Angel 123
Her Word of Reproach 124
Caprice at Home 125
A Ghost at the Opera 127
A Lesson in a Picture 129
After the Quarrel 131
"To Be Dead" 133
The Baby's Brother 134
One Year Old 135
Child's-Faith 136
The Sight of Trouble 137
A Hint of Homer (Their Heroic Lesson) 139

From <u>An Irish Garland</u> (1885):

In Clonmel Parish Churchyard 140
   (At the Grave of Charles Wolfe)
A Call on Sir Walter Raleigh 141
A Child's Cry 143
Comfort through a Window 144

From <u>The Children Out-of-Doors</u> (1885):

The Thought of Astyanax beside Iulus 145
A Neighbourhood Incident 146
His Mother's Way 148
In Street and Garden (I) (A Child's Conclusion) 150
The Christening 151

From <u>In Primrose Time</u> (1886):

A Portrait at Youghal 152
Two Innocents Abroad 153

From <u>The Witch in the Glass</u> (1889):

The Witch in the Glass 155
The Sermon of a Statue 156
After Her First Party 157
A Triumph of Travel 159
The Story of a Storm 160
The Coming Out of Her Doll 161
Requiescat (Lie Still) 162
At the Grave of a Suicide 163
The Night-Moth's Comment 164

From <u>An Irish Wild-Flower</u> (1891):

An Irish Wild-Flower 165
From an Ancient Mound 166
A Word with a Skylark 167
His Argument 168
Carrigaline Castle 169
In the Round Tower at Cloyne 171
Last of His Line 172
Pro Patria 174

From <u>Child's-World Ballads</u> (1895):

A Sea-Gull Wounded 176
Confession 177

Uncollected Poems from Periodicals:

Giving Back the Flower (<u>Galaxy</u>, 1867) 178
A Hundred Years Ago (<u>Galaxy</u>, 1870) 180
Shoulder-Rank (<u>The Capital</u>, 1871) 181
One from the Dead (<u>Overland Monthly</u>, 1871) 182
Another War (<u>The Capital</u>, 1872) 184
Mock Diamonds (<u>The Capital</u>, 1872) 186
The Sorrows of Charlotte (<u>The Capital</u>, 1872) 188
The Grave at Frankfort (<u>The Capital</u>, 1872) 189

Her Blindness in Grief (<u>Independent</u>, 1873) 190

Worthless Treasure   (<u>The Capital</u>, 1875)   192

A Child's Party   (<u>Wide-Awake</u>, 1883)   194

To Frances Cleveland   (<u>Belford's</u>, 1888)   199

"Some Sweetest Mouth on Earth..."   201
   (Tynan, from c. 1888)

Inspiration and Poem (<u>Bookman</u>, 1897)   202

Happiness (A Butterfly) (<u>Harper's Monthly</u>, 1897) 203

A Mistake in the Bird-Market (<u>Century</u>, 1898)   204

A Prayer to Osiris (<u>Hesperian Tree</u>, 1900)   205

A Shadowy Third   (<u>Hesperian Tree</u>, 1903)   206

A Woman's No   (<u>Hesperian Tree</u>, 1903)   207

The Coming-Back of the Dead (<u>Hesperian Tree</u>, 1903) ... 208

All in the Bud and Bloom 'o the Year   209
   (<u>Harper's Monthly</u>, 1909)

A New Thanksgiving (<u>Independent</u>, 1910) 210

A Daffodil   (<u>Independent</u>, 1911)   211

Notes   212

Bibliography of Publications by Sarah Piatt 235
Including Reviews

Bibliography of Biographical and Critical 261
References to Sarah Piatt

Index of Titles   267

SARAH M. B. PIATT.

INTRODUCTION

In her recent anthology, <u>Nineteenth-Century American Women Writers</u>, Karen Kilcup calls Sarah Piatt "a forgotten writer, misread as a domestic poet in her own day, whose work should be read alongside that of Walt Whitman and Dickinson as one of the preeminent poets in nineteenth-century American literature." Paula Bernat Bennett, introducing Piatt in her fine <u>Nineteenth-Century American Women Poets</u> anthology, writes: "After Emily Dickinson, Piatt is arguably the most difficult and, at the same time, most rewarding woman poet writing in America in the course of the century."

Given the thoroughness of modern literary scholarship, it is remarkable how Piatt's work could have been so completely lost. Writing in the last half of the nineteenth century, she created a major body of poetry that needs to be rescued from oblivion and read again today. An intelligent, powerful, and complex poet, she has been neglected too long.

* * *

Sarah Morgan Bryan was born near Lexington, Kentucky, on August 11, 1836, the older of two daughters of Mary (Spiers) and Talbot Nelson Bryan. Her Bryan ancestors were associated back in North Carolina with the Boone family. Rebecca Bryan, the niece of Sarah's great-grandfather, William Bryan, became the wife of Daniel Boone. In 1720, Squire Boone, Daniel's father, had married Sarah Morgan, for whom the poet was named. The two families moved to Kentucky in the 1770s and established Bryan's Station (later incorporated by Lexington), a pioneer outpost prominent in the Indian wars of that time. Sarah's mother was also related to other early Kentucky families, the Stocktons and the Simpsons.

When Sarah was three years old, her family moved a few miles west of Lexington to Versailles, Woodford County, Kentucky, where her "lovely and beautiful" mother died in 1844. For the next

9

few years Sarah and her sister Ellen lived first with their maternal grandmother at Lexington, then with family friends near Versailles, and later for a short time with their father and wealthy step-mother. Living on these slave-owning plantations helped shape Piatt's complex views about slavery and the Civil War which would appear in many of her poems. Finally, her father "placed" her with his sister, Mrs. Annie Boone, at New Castle, where she graduated from the fashionable Henry Female College in 1854. The loss of her mother when she was only eight and the subsequent moves are said to have contributed to her characteristic reserve and the "darker side" of her nature.

She possessed a girlish charm and was remembered as a "delicate and graceful" young woman with hazel eyes and auburn hair. She also had a quiet dignity and modesty that endeared her to other writers and political figures she would meet as an adult. From the stresses of her childhood she developed an inner strength and stamina that sustained her through the loss of at least three children and the financial difficulties of her married life. Sadness and playfulness are inseparable in her poems.

As a young girl, Sallie Bryan was thoroughly familiar with the foremost English poets of her day, especially Shelley, Byron (whom George Prentice chastises her for imitating), and Coleridge. Her poems, such as "Aunt Annie" and "The Black Princess," provide the only existing glimpses of her childhood feelings. By chance, a cousin showed one of her early poems to a Texas editor who printed it in his paper, the Galveston News. Soon her work was discovered by George Prentice, editor of the Louisville Journal, who thought she would become "the leading woman poet in America." He printed dozens of her poems in his newspaper during the 1850s. Other papers printed her poems as well, and by 1860 she was well known throughout Kentucky.

Also through Prentice she met another of his proteges, the Ohio poet John James Piatt. Nothing is recorded of their courtship, but they were married in New Castle, at her Aunt Annie's house, on June 18, 1861. Jean Allen Hanawalt, in her 1981 dissertation, gives Stoddard's contemporary description of Sarah at the time of her marriage as "slightly above the average height for a woman, very graceful in carriage and figure. Her head [was] singularly fine in shape and outline [with] dark, tender, hazel eyes under finely arched eyebrows, a small, sensitive and proud mouth, a straight, well-shaped nose." Soon after the wedding, John took her to live in Washington DC, where he had been appointed a clerk in the U.S. Treasury Department. Life must have looked very promising for the young couple.

Their first home was in Woodley, Georgetown, about a mile from the White House. John's friend William Dean Howells often stayed with them, and in Washington they also met John Burroughs and Walt Whitman. Another friend John made was the anthologist Edmund C. Stedman, who wrote to Howells that "Piatt and his Sallie are snug in their Georgetown cottage." A month after their marriage, Sarah wrote a poem about the defeated Union Army fleeing back to Washington after the first Battle of Bull Run. In 1862 their first child, Marian Prentice, arrived, the only daughter followed eventually by six sons. Also during this time, they published their first book together, The Nests at Washington, in 1864, the year their first son Victor was born.

By 1867, John's appointment in Washington had run its course, and the family looked to the west, choosing to settle in North Bend, Ohio, near Cincinnati. There they built a story-and-a-half "cottage" with French windows on ten acres with a sweeping view a hundred feet above the Ohio River. President William Henry Harrison's tomb, mentioned in one of Sarah's child-poems, was a quarter mile from their home. From 1870 to 1876, John was back in Washington as librarian of the House of Representatives. Sarah and the children joined him there during the winters, but spent their summers at home in North Bend. Some of the poems from this time express her bitterness at their separation.

The family grew and overflowed the house, and many of Sarah's poems for and about children date from this period and reflect both her joy at being a mother and her deep compassion. Marian and Victor were followed by Donn (1867), Fred (1869), Guy (1871), Louis (1875), and Cecil (1878). Although happy at

"Riverbrow," the large family had financial worries, as John struggled to make a living by writing for newspapers and publishing volumes of their poems. He worked hard and knew many people, but never received the important position (like Howells at the Atlantic) that would have provided for the family, and so had to depend on uncertain government appointments. John did unselfishly promote Sarah's poetry, with little help from her, sending it for publication in books and periodicals, even when her fame began to eclipse his own. Although Sarah expressed bitterness about marriage in many poems, their mutual bond remained strong, and other poems like John's "To a Lady" and Sarah's "My Wedding Ring" show a playfulness and affection that remained. (For more details about the Piatt's home, see Farman and Stoddard.)

The family, like many of that period, was touched by tragedy. Victor, the beloved oldest son, was killed suddenly before her eyes in a fireworks explosion on July 4th, 1874, an accident particularly devastating to Sarah. Another son, Louis, was drowned in a boating accident in 1884 during the Piatts' stay in Ireland. These great losses appear often in her poems, as do the apparent loss of other children in infancy or through miscarriage. Certainly, her love for children and her feelings about death are constant themes in the poems.

On June 3, 1882, the family sailed from New York to begin a long residence in Ireland, where John served as United States Consul at Cork until 1893. There Sarah continued to write many new poems, made a growing circle of literary friendships, and began to attract wide and favorable notice. Several new poetry volumes were published in these years, and some of the flavor of the family's life in Ireland was also preserved in details recorded in a few delightful prose pieces. In 1893, the family moved from Queenstown when John was promoted to a new position in Dublin. That job, however, lasted only a few months, and then the family moved to London for a year before returning permanently to the United States in 1894.

After spending some time in Washington where John worked again for the House of Representatives, they finally were settled back at North Bend by 1898. Their last years at "Riverbrow" were troubled by more financial worries, and John jokingly wished that they "could live on views where there were no prospects." Their cottage burned down, but they rebuilt it in the style of their Irish home at Queenstown. Also, John edited two collections of Ohio Valley writing called The Hesperian Tree, published in 1900 and 1903, but no more volumes of their own poetry appeared and their magazine publications decreased. In 1914, John was nearly paralyzed in a carriage accident, and Howells sought help for them from the Author's Club Fund.

John died quietly on February 16, 1917, and Sarah then moved to Caldwell, New Jersey, to live with her youngest son Cecil who was in the fire insurance business. She died there on December 22, 1919, at the age of 83.

The Late 19th Century Literary Climate for Women

Piatt wrote in an era that was in many ways favorable to women poets, but which also contributed to the neglect of her work. The last half of the nineteenth century saw more women writers break into print than at any previous time in literary history. Yet thirty years later, as Bennett writes, "the names and contributions of almost all of these women...would be lost. From the stand-point of United States literary history, for most of the twentieth century, it has been as if they never wrote, never were." Only within the last few years, particularly in the wake of Cheryl Walker's landmark anthology, has this whole era of women's writing been seriously reconsidered. An understanding of Piatt's own late nineteenth-century cultural and literary climate is therefore necessary to compare her poetry with that of her contemporaries and show how in many ways it surpasses the other poetry of her time.

Extensively published and critically applauded during her lifetime, Piatt never escaped the late nineteenth-century label of "poetess," those second-class citizens of literature praised condescendingly by male critics as "sweet singers" who were seldom given a serious reading. Howells (with good intentions) wrote a review of her book <u>A Woman's Poems</u> in the Atlantic (July 1871), in which he uses the adjectives "delicate," "thoroughly feminine," "lovely," and "womanly." He goes on to say:

> In whatever women write there is apt to be feeling enough, but in what Mrs. Piatt writes there is thought, too; not always the strongest or the greatest, and sometimes rather too closely veiled, but thought nevertheless, and uttered in a manner quite her own.

Such condescending praise clearly classes Piatt and other women poets as women first and poets second. Although they enjoyed wide publication and popular readership (largely among women), these nineteenth-century poets never had an equal chance to enter the enduring rolls of the American literary canon.

Piatt had much in common with other women writers of her day. In her provocative book <u>The Nightingale's Burden: Women Poets and American Culture before 1900</u>, Walker sketches a composite biography that fits many of the women who published poetry and prose during the nineteenth century. Drawing on the lives of Maria Brooks, Lucretia Davidson, Lydia Sigourney, Frances Osgood, Elizabeth Oakes-Smith, Lucy Larcom, and Frances Harper, supplemented by several others, Walker discusses their shared experiences.

All these poets were considered precocious and many published very young. The fascination with the inspired "child-poet," which can be seen as late as the 1920s in Hilda Conkling and Nathalia Crane, was typified by the popularity of Davidson, who wrote many of her poems at the age of fourteen and died in 1825 just before her seventeenth birthday. Mark Twain satirizes such poetry in Huck Finn's description of the poor, dead poetess Emmeline Grangerford, who "could make poetry like that before she was fourteen," and who "didn't ever have to stop and think," but "could write about anything you choose to give her to write about, just so it was sadful." Emma Lazarus and Harper also wrote and later published poetry while still in their teens, and Rose Terry Cooke wrote poems and plays. In fact, unless a girl showed literary promise at an early age, it was more difficult for her to find a publisher later in her career. Piatt was published in the Louisville Journal as early as 1855, soon after turning nineteen. Before her mid-20s, she was well known throughout the state of Kentucky. Yet none of the over one hundred surviving poems written before her marriage can be considered as more than interesting juvenilia.

Similarly, women poets were thought of and encouraged to be artless amateurs. Rufus Griswold, the influential anthologist, praises Osgood because "her poems cost her as little effort or reflection as the epigram or touching sentiment that summoned laughter or tears to the group about her in the drawing room." Poems of Anne Lynch (later Botta) are referred to as "unpremeditated effusions." Although she never revised her poems once they had appeared in print, Piatt's intensity and ruthless honesty were not the "effusions" of an amateur, and their technical skill and complexity suggest (though no known manuscripts exist) careful composition.

The women poets of this time were often associated at a young age with strong male figures. Poe was a mentor to many female poets, such as Sarah Helen Whitman and Frances Osgood. Whittier influenced the careers and promoted the poems of Lucy Larcom, Sarah Whitman, Alice Cary, Ina Coolbrith, and Celia Thaxter. Lowell, Holmes, Emerson, Higginson, and others also served as mentors, as did the anthologists Griswold and Stedman. Piatt had several supportive male figures, beginning with George Prentice. Her husband also supported her career, unlike the husbands of many of her contemporaries, such as Lydia Sigourney, Osgood, Elizabeth Oakes-Smith, and Julia Ward Howe. Piatt also enjoyed the patronage of her husband's long-time friend, William Dean Howells, who reviewed A Woman's Poems, published twenty-three of her poems while he was editor of the Atlantic, and published five more while in the "Editor's Easy Chair" at Harper's. But the help these men offered to Piatt and other women poets, however sincere, often was at root condescending toward, in Stedman's phrase, "the tuneful sisterhood."

Young women, especially as the century progressed, also enjoyed more opportunities to receive an education, even if largely segregated at women's schools. Both Bennett and Walker mention the shift in attitudes toward more advanced learning for women, and a number of private seminaries, such as the Emma Willard School in Troy, New York, Mount Holyoke Female Seminary, and the Hartford Female Seminary, flourished. Most of the better-known poets of the time received at least some advanced instruction in classical literature, European languages, geography, and mathematics. Emma Lazarus was not only taught several languages, but also traveled extensively in Europe. While at Henry Female Seminary, Piatt received a strong grounding in the Greek classics and in Romantic literature. Her poems also indicate familiarity with Shakespeare and wide reading in history.

Perhaps the most significant change that affected women's writing in the nineteenth century was the number of periodicals that opened their pages to them. Fred Lewis Pattee, in A History of American Literature Since 1870, categorized the poems published in the Atlantic Monthly during the decade of the 1870s. Longfellow, Holmes, Whittier, Lowell, and Aldrich accounted for 108 of them, but of the 450 other poems that appeared in the magazine, 201 were written by women. Although they published in great numbers, women were still excluded from what Janet Gray calls "the collegial networks among publishers, critics and academics through which enduring reputations, and thus literary canons, are made." Also, some male writers resented the attention given this (in Hawthorne's famous phrase) "damned mob of scribbling women," and discounted their work. Yet, there was certainly no question about their popularity. Piatt published about one hundred poems in major periodicals, such as Harper's, Atlantic, Scribner's, Independent, Appleton's, Century, and Galaxy, approximately the same number as her contemporaries like Louise Chandler Moulton and Celia Thaxter, and twice as many as her husband.

The income these women poets received from such publications was often needed by their families, and it gave them an even greater incentive to write. Financial inducement, however, often led them to write for the popular market rather than for purely literary expression. Early in the century, Sigourney complained of the "slight themes that were desired," yet was paid as much as $100 for four poems and, beginning in 1840, was given $500 a year by Louis Godey just for her name to appear on the title page of his Lady's Book. Her husband, Charles, resented her success, as did the husbands of Oakes-Smith, Howe, Cooke, and Thaxter, but they all took the money. Sigourney, the Cary sisters, Howe, Frances Harper, Lucy Larcom, and Ella Wheeler Wilcox all earned significant incomes from their poetry. Gray points out, however, that "selling enough books to support oneself and being praised by critics as a true poet became almost mutually exclusive." Piatt, for the most part, was indifferent to the fate of her poems, and wrote to please herself rather than soften her work to appease popular taste. Poems such as "Marble or Dust?," "The Order for Her Portrait," "Her Cross and Mine," "Requiescat," "If I Were a Queen," "A Dead Man's Friends," and "The Fancy Ball" all show her disdain toward the "admiring bog." John James, however, who expended much effort to place her poems, must have had at least one eye on monetary return. This may be why some of her best work, which is rough, angry, and shockingly honest compared with John James' own conventional poetry (what Bennett calls "a constant ironic deconstruction of what J.J. and much of his society held dear"), was never published in the leading magazines or (in some cases) even included in any of her books.

Because of their access to magazine publication and better communications in general, these women were aware of each other's work and came to rely on their sister poets for support and encouragement. Women corresponded extensively with one another, read one another's work, and participated in a number of famous literary salons. The New York salon hosted by Anne Lynch was attended by Poe, Emerson, Osgood, Griswold, Oakes-Smith, the Cary sisters, and Margaret Fuller. Edith Thomas's career was launched there by a reading she gave one evening. Other well-known salons were conducted by Emma Embury, Celia Thaxter (for thirty summers on her beloved Appledore Island), and Ina Coolbrith (in Oakland and San Francisco). These networks of connections were invaluable to women writers who otherwise could have been isolated by domineering husbands and pressing family responsibilities. Piatt, however, seems to have taken less interest in such literary networks than her husband, but she did cultivate friendships with writers while in Ireland and corresponded with Louise Chandler Moulton and other women poets.

In spite of their success in publishing large numbers of poems and their familiarity with one another's work, women were expected to confine themselves to certain generally-accepted themes. Walker discusses these "themes deemed appropriate to feminine life," such as events resulting in religious consolation, love of nature and the passing seasons, noble deeds, domestic joys and sorrows, sickness and death, and of course all the moods of love. Conflicting desires can be seen in categories Walker labels the "free-bird poem" (escape) and the "sanctuary poem" (safe haven). Other categories include the "power fantasy," the "secret sorrow," and the "forbidden lover" poem. Also, a well-developed Victorian "language of gems" and "language of flowers" allowed women poets to express subtleties of moods and feelings through an elaborately encoded symbolism. Yet, in no way, as Walker writes, "was a woman poet (any more than a man) expected to provide serious political, social, or religious challenges to the status quo." Women often resorted to dreams or exotic settings to camouflage their more daring feelings or subject matter. However, Bennett argues that a number of women were breaking new ground and writing about subjects as "modern" as abortion, sexual abuse, unwed motherhood, the advantages of not marrying, breast-feeding, all types of sexual passion, negative feelings about marriage and children, incest, the fate of the homeless, the oppression of African Americans, the decimation of Native Americans, and doubts about the accepted religious truths. Bennett writes in the introduction to her anthology that "by the time I finished collecting poems for this volume, I was persuaded that there was nothing nineteenth-century women poets did not write on." And certainly Piatt, both in style and thematic content, often went far beyond the acceptable boundaries of nineteenth-century genteel taste expected of a woman poet, writing about many of the above themes in complex ways with an anger and intensity often heightened by irony or dramatic tension.

In fact, the nineteenth century saw the gradual breakdown of many of the conventions regarding women and society. Coventry Patmore's The Angel in the House (1854) expressed an idealized view of women repeated in countless poems throughout the century that tried to make all women into a type of domestic angel. In her stimulating essay, "'The Descent of the Angel': Interrogating Domestic Ideology in American Women's Poetry, 1858-1890," Bennett traces the decline of the romantic ideal of transforming female spirituality as these women poets were confronted by the grim realities of nineteenth-century marriage and domestic life. In her explication of Piatt's "Descent," Bennett writes: "Far from leading her husband to heaven, as Patmore's speaker insists the Angel/Wife does, Piatt's bride is herself immersed in the everyday. Possessed of house and keys, she is possessed by them." Although the sentimental stereotype of the domestic ideal would continue to be expressed throughout the century, women writers like Piatt were beginning to assert that it could in many cases be destructive to women socially, financially, and psychologically. Many of Piatt's darker poems express her outrage at being a "slave of the ring."

The domestic ideal increasingly was viewed in a harsher light because so many nineteenth-century women writers became trapped in loveless marriages to despotic husbands who were jealous of their success. Walker writes in The Nightingale's Burden: "Marriage and duty are often synonymous for these women, and both at times represent self-sacrifice and suffering." Among the first wave of poets, Sigourney, Brooks, and Oakes-Smith were married young to much older men who proved unsatisfactory husbands. Oakes-Smith, in particular, was married at sixteen to a man twice her age who was physically unattractive to her and who discouraged her writing while he himself went bankrupt. In 1842 she had published "The Sinless Child," a long poem that epitomized the romantic ideal of the innocence of womanhood, but by the 1850s she was deeply involved in the woman's movement, speaking and writing about the need for sweeping domestic reforms. Osgood, Howe, Cooke, and Thaxter also had unhappy to disastrous marriages. Cooke, after much success, at forty-six married a man sixteen years younger who spent her into genteel poverty and severely blighted her literary career. A few marriages, those of Embury, Moulton, and

Harriet Prescott Spofford, were healthy and productive, but several other women poets, like Larcom, Alice and Phoebe Cary, Dickinson, Thomas, Lizette Woodworth Reese, and Imogen Louise Guiney, chose to remain single. Piatt's marriage was better than most. She wrote more than a few poems that reflected a genuine love for her husband. John James also did much to promote her poetry, and tried hard to advance his own career beyond what his meager talents allowed. Piatt enjoyed her children and many aspects of her domestic life at Riverbrow as well as in Washington or Ireland. Yet many of her poems chafe at the limitations and privations of marriage, at her husband's emotional distance to her and her children, and at their perpetual financial worries.

Walker summarizes her composite biography: "One of the patterns most frequently repeated in these poets' biographies is precocity, adolescent distinction, marriage, followed by disillusionment and years of difficult adjustment to an unpalatable wifely role." Though well-educated and offered access to wide publication at an early age, these women experienced many frustrations in their marriages and domestic lives, as well as with the confinements and limitations that society placed upon them and their writing. Yet they produced a startlingly diverse body of work that is only beginning to be seriously examined again today. Sarah Piatt's life and career in many ways followed the same pattern as that of her contemporaries. She experienced the sweeping changes the nineteenth century brought into the lives of women and to the whole fabric of society. When the first reformers were meeting at Seneca Falls in 1848, Piatt was a twelve-year-old girl from a prominent southern family who had lost her idealized mother and was now living with slave-owning relatives. By the time of her death at the age of eighty-three, she had lived most of her life north of the Ohio River, experienced the Civil War up close in Washington DC, mothered at least eight living children of whom five reached maturity and only three survived her, had seen the end of the frontier, witnessed shocking cruelty to Native Americans, African Americans, and the poor, spent more than a decade across the ocean, and lived to see the end of the First World War. Yet she missed by one year the opportunity to vote in a national election. Piatt was a woman of her time, but like the best of her contemporaries, her poetry pushed beyond the boundaries and limitations of her age.

Piatt's Poetry in a Neglected Age

Why has the work of nineteenth-century American women poets, except for Emily Dickinson's, been so utterly lost, and what sets Piatt's poetry apart from that of most other writers of the time? These overlapping questions must be addressed in any serious consideration of Piatt.

Throughout most of the twentieth century, little attention has been paid to the immense number of nineteenth-century poems collected into hundreds of volumes running often to two or three hundred pages each. Or, even if read, the work of these poets is discounted. Bennett remarks, "No group of writers in United States literary history has been subject to more consistent denigration than nineteenth-century women, especially the poets." Walker, in The Nightingale's Burden, writes about nineteenth-century poetry in general: "Read as poetry, the lack of compression, of originality, the rareness of fresh insight or humor in women's poems are disturbing." She concludes: "On the whole, this body of work defies reassessment. The critical standards it invokes are so invariably those of its own time that one feels anachronistic in applauding or condemning it. These poems are not alive to the possibility of contemporary renewals: their language is too stilted, their convictions too predictable, their rhythms too monotonous." Lumped together as sentimental and hopelessly dated, the work of all these poets was dismissed from the canon of American literature as a whole.

But, it must be asked, is this general condemnation justified in light of such a large and diverse body of writing? Already by the 1850s, what Bennett calls the "High Sentimentalism" of forerunners like Sigourney, Oakes-Smith, and Osgood was being challenged by the next generation of poets. Even though most of these women were writing for the popular press, they still addressed a broad range of subjects and by the latter part of the century were publishing

21

poems that openly defied the conventional views expected of women. To be published, any writer will be influenced by the aesthetic ethos of his or her time, yet these poets, writing in an era of strictly proscribed metrical standards, were able to bring humor, irony, tragedy, parody, and satire into their poems. The excellent parodies of Phoebe Cary are an example of a poet being successful in one style even though much of her other work is ordinary. In addition, some late-century poets, such as Edith Thomas, were writing poems with sharp, clear imagery that have been seen as forerunners to modernist poetry.

It is also unfair to these poets that they have come to be judged almost solely in comparison with Dickinson. Her poetry burst on the scene just as popular taste was changing at the end of the century, and the strategy ever since has been to play her off against other poets to emphasize her genius at their expense. Also, as modernism was beginning to rout almost all Victorian and Georgian poetry during the dark days of World War I, anthologies were starting to emphasize only the "great" poets rather than collect the work of a larger number of representative poets. A comparison of Stedman's comprehensive anthology of 1900 with the later selective anthologies of Louis Untermeyer or Oscar Williams illustrates this growing exclusivity. Gray writes that "Dickinson's status was secured as a distinctly modern poetics gained authority, an approach to poetic evaluation centered on the notions that a poet is an exceptionally gifted person who rises above the literary marketplace and that poetry is a discipline unto itself, answerable only to its own formal rules." Therefore nineteenth-century poets were no longer read according to the cultural ethos and the aesthetics of their own time, and the great majority of them did not measure up to "modern" standards, especially when compared with such gifted but isolated poets as Whitman, Hopkins in England, and Dickinson.

The sharp contrast of modernism, which broke with the generally accepted fundamentals of poetry, together with the growing tendency to anthologize only poets of the highest stature, sounded the death knell for most nineteenth-century poetry. The poetry and criticism of Pound and Eliot, followed by the influential work of poets such as Yeats, Williams, Stevens, and Auden, came to dominate the taste and opinion of the new century. Free verse replaced regular metronomic meters, while at the same time obvious and predictable rhymes were discarded in favor of the precise word and image. Critics discussed the difficult and obscure poem, but saw easily-accessible poetry that celebrated traditional religious or patriotic themes as old-fashioned and naive. Women poets especially were seen as overly emotional, timid, and simplistic as the modern world grappled with the horrors of world war and a fragmented society. Even the vastly-popular "fireside poets" (Longfellow, Whittier, Holmes, Bryant) were denigrated or seen as merely representative of an outdated era. By the 1920s, only the "greats:" Whitman, Dickinson, and perhaps a bit of Poe and Emerson were considered truly canonical from the nineteenth century in American poetry.

However, in the 1990s a new interest has developed in nineteenth-century women's writing. Several comprehensive anthologies have been published, Legacy: A Journal of Nineteenth-Century American Women Writers has become an important source, and other attempts at a re-evaluation have begun. The current perspective is more aware of the limits of modernism and has shown an increased interest in reading the best poetry in the context of its own age. For centuries, poetry has been a vehicle for passing along to future generations the oral traditions and experiences of any community or people in the most profound and moving way possible. Nineteenth-century writers gave voice to the zeitgeist of their own time, just as twentieth-century poets had to find a new way to express their age. Women poets of the nineteenth century, in particular, were struggling with historic changes that would profoundly affect their place in society and their role within the family. Writers like Piatt are rewarding and surprising because they were able to convey their era with intelligence and feeling in a significant number of poems and in a wide range of voices and content.

Sarah Piatt's poetry is remarkable for several reasons, particularly for her distinctive voice, her dramatic tension, and for her complexity. Even when read for the first time, the poems convey a sense of immediacy. The reader hears the voice of a real person. According to Alicia Ostriker, "When a woman poet says 'I' she is likely to mean the actual 'I' as intensely as her verbal skills admit." This is particularly true of Piatt, even when she is writing from the point of view of a child, a historic character, or even a man. The emotion she feels, especially in the poems about her own life, is expressed as directly and honestly as if the real woman were addressing the reader in person. Emerson Venable calls her poetry "simply the bitter truth," and says that "the reader need not be told that such poems were lived before they were written." He quotes a reviewer from the Pictorial World (London): "Mrs. Piatt studies no model, and takes no pattern for her work; she simply expresses herself; hence her verse is just the transparent mantle of her individuality." Many poems, such as "Shapes of a Soul," "The Order for Her Portrait," and "The Fancy Ball," emphasize her uncompromising individuality regardless of what others may expect from her. "The Fancy Ball" ends with the lines:

> ...Hush: if I go at all,
> (It will make them stare and shrink,
> It will look so strange at a Fancy Ball),
> I will go as--Myself, I think!

Piatt's voice is authentic. Andrei Codrescu, a modern Romanian-born poet, has stated that the "poetic has always been the enemy of poetry." Piatt does not keep a safe "poetic distance" from her subject, but in her best work probes with complex imagery the almost Robert Frost-like darker side of her nature and the stubborn paradoxes of the human situation, expressing genuine emotion and thought rather than merely composing a poem. Kilcup writes, "Piatt transforms ostensibly conventional themes with a searingly dark and ironic voice." She certainly did not always deliver the proper "poetic" sentiment about a given subject. The death of a child was a conventional topic for woman poets of the time, but Piatt brings an honesty and intensity seldom found in such poems about little angels now at peace. In her poem "No Help," when she says "And do I want a little angel? No,/I want my baby," she means it. And when she confronts the hollow popular consolation "Is he not with his Father/...Is he not His?" she concludes, "Was he not also mine?" and

"Think you, to give my bosom back his breath/I would not kiss him from the peace called death?" And she means that also. There is no topic she hesitates to explore, whether marriage or family or love or death, and her characteristic honesty and directness are apparent, sometimes with a light touch and sometimes with dark bitterness (and sometimes with both), in poems like "A Pique at Parting," "Giving Back the Flower," "Leaving Love," "The Grave at Frankfort," "Happiness (A Butterfly)," "Her Word of Reproach," "The Sorrows of Charlotte," "The Palace-Burner," and "Beatrice Cenci."

Piatt is also directly and immediately involved with her subject. So much poetry of the time was simply a long build-up to a pre-conceived moral or clever observation, but Piatt creates an interest in her subject as she thinks her way through the poem rather than let the poem dictate her thought. Piatt's voice often comes through clearest in her poems with children. Many poets idealized childhood (Longfellow) or reminisced about it (Whittier), but Piatt actually talks with children and explores their feelings. Instead of teaching a lesson or sentimentalizing a moment, she, according to Hanawalt, "achieves a conversational quality all her own." For example, in Margaret Junkin Preston's poem about a first snowfall, the child sees such beauty and concludes, "We have gone to heaven." But Piatt's poem "A Child's First Sight of Snow" ends: "Little wordless Questioner--'What does it mean?'/Why, it means, that the world is cold." Here Piatt uses cold in both senses, and it is possible that she is subtly mocking pretentious poems like Preston's as well. She also can soften otherwise harsh social commentary by speaking it from a child's point of view, such as her son's conclusion in "His Argument" about the ruler who does nothing for his people:

> 'What I will do is--nothing! Don't you see?
> Then I'll have everything, my whole life through.
> But if I work, why I might always be
> Living in huts with gold flowers on them, too--
> And half a door. And that won't do for me.'

Piatt often puts her own words in the mouths of children, usually to reveal a bitter or ironic truth, but the poems still succeed in capturing the essential interaction between two real children or between a mother and her child.

When compared with other poets of her time, Piatt employs a surprisingly wide variety of styles and voices. Irony is common. "A New Thanksgiving" is even an ironic prayer. Unflinching self-appraisal is pervasive, especially in such dark poems as "Her Blindness in Grief," "The Palace-Burner," "Death before Death," "A Woman's Birthday," "Shapes of a Soul," and "The Descent of the Angel." Yet there is also broad humor in such poems as "Two Innocents Abroad" (which shows a reading of Twain) and "Last of His Line." Piatt is even capable of poking fun at her own tendency to brood in "Caprice at Home" and "Sweetness of Bitterness."

Her poems with children are indicative of her stylistic range. Even though these poems are full of gentle humor and playfulness and show her genuine love for children, they also contain a great deal of her darker side. Brooding about a lost child makes her more distant from her living children ("Sad Wisdom--Four Years Old"). The loss of her children's need for her as they grow up is compared to losing them through actual death ("My Babes in the Wood"). The inevitable loss of childhood innocence appears in "The Witch in the Glass" and "More About Fairies." And as a mother she knows her children will have to face failure ("Crying for the Moon") and even death ("The Funeral of a Doll"). Even in the delightfully playful "After Her First Party," there is a sadness as the mother thinks about an early love who is now dead, all the while her daughter is blissfully unaware of the fact. This pervasive darkness went unnoticed by Piatt's reviewers, but coupled with her humor and irony, it gives these poems a power and poignancy unmatched in her day.

Another aspect of her poetry that distinguishes it from the work of her contemporaries is the heightened drama she achieves, not just through use of dialogue, but through a dialogic tension that develops and explores contrasting viewpoints. The tension can be between mother and child, husband and wife, or universal questions of faith and doubt, but Piatt is able to develop that tension naturally within the poem. Bennett writes, "Rooting her poetry in the social world, she mediates her themes through dialogue instead, letting the moments she depicts stand as they are, for readers to do with as they may. Like Dickinson's poetry, therefore, Piatt's demands that one interact with it to read it at all." Sometimes she uses direct dialogue, sometimes rhetorical questions, and sometimes merely implies another view ("I was thinking of things that were sad to me--/There, hush! you know nothing about them, Kate."), but the dramatic tension she creates is unusually effective and heightens the reader's interest in the poem.

The tensions in her poetry come from the dramatic tensions in her own life. She came to maturity in the bitter and difficult decade before the Civil War, living on the border between North and South in the Lexington-to-Cincinnati axis that inspired Stowe to write Uncle Tom's Cabin while Piatt was in her teens. Poems like "A Child's Party" and "The Black Princess" express her conflicted feelings about slavery at that time. Her marriage in 1861 took her across the Ohio River for the rest of her life, put her in Washington DC in the middle of the war, and uprooted her from her deep antebellum roots. She looks back in such moving poems as "Over in Kentucky" at her "two worlds" now divided and forever changed. Early lovers and irreconcilable loyalties are cast against a background of the terrible slaughter and stark reality of war, producing a significant number of powerful poems: "Giving Back the Flower," "The Grave at Frankfort," "Mock Diamonds," "A Hundred Years Ago," "There Was a Rose," "Hearing the Battle," "Another War," "Shoulder-Rank," "Army of Occupation," and others. Because of their first-hand experience of the war and characteristic honesty, Piatt's war poems deserve to be better known.

Death was a constant tension in her life, beginning with the early loss of her mother. Piatt also lost former suitors during the war, at least one infant, and two of her beloved young boys. Dozens of her darker poems reflect her struggle to cope with these devastating deaths of loved ones. She can never quite fully come to trust "That New World" offered by religious consolation and attested to by her children in such poems as "Child's Faith," "In Street and Garden (A Child's Conclusion)," and "Calling the Dead." Her completely honest and prolonged wrestling with death and loss

27

gives her poetry much of its poignancy and power, while helping her avoid easy answers and shallow moralizing. It also enables her to feel genuine empathy for the suffering of others, as in "Aunt Annie," "Their Two Fortunes," "The Thought of Astyanax beside Iulus," and her many poems about beggars. This profound empathy is one of the strengths of her work. Even in her lighter vein, when dealing with the loss of childhood illusions (fairyland) and the loss of her own youth and beauty, she generally rises above mere sentimentality through her ironic humor.

There was also tension in her marriage. Her husband's emotional superficiality (reflected in his poetry) she dramatically portrays in poems like "Her Word of Reproach." His consolation comes too easily and is of little help to her in her search for spiritual and psychological comfort. Because he does not understand the complexities of her nature, she often turns to the deeply sympathetic relationship she has with her children to work out her internal struggles. Her husband not only uprooted her from her childhood, but also from her home-life with her own children. Although travel could be exciting, she tired of living in Washington DC, often spending part of the year back in North Bend, and she grew homesick in Ireland, as seen in poems like "A Word with a Skylark" and "Pro Patria." Because of their large and growing family, financial difficulties also caused tension in the Piatts' marriage. Many poems, such as "Gaslight and Starlight" and "This World," have their roots in the struggle to reconcile her unrequited love of material possessions with the higher values of charity and unselfishness. In a significant number of remarkable poems Piatt was able to dramatize all these tensions inherent in her life.

It is possible that she has written the best dramatic monologues (and dialogues) between those of Robert Browning and Frost's North of Boston. Piatt has the same knack for catching the nuances of ordinary speech and the technical skill for working them naturally into tight metrical patterns. In "The Palace-Burner," for example, the mother's subtle mood changes and the progression of her thinking is engagingly told in nine compact stanzas of iambic pentameter closely rhymed a-b-a-b. Through her use of enjambment and the short sentences natural to conversation, Piatt's rhymes never become intrusive, as in:

> You would have burned the palace? Just because
> You did not live in it yourself! Oh! why?
> Have I not taught you to respect the laws?
> *You* would have burned the palace. Would not *I*?
>
> Would I? Go to your play. Would I, indeed?
> *I*? Does the boy not know my soul to be
> Languid and worldly, with a dainty need
> For light and music? Yet he questions me.

Not until Frost, would such a natural voice come from such tightly controlled stanzas. But Piatt also clearly conveys the mother's innermost thoughts as the conversation with her son develops. The boy is drawn to the two-year-old picture in a newspaper showing the execution of a lady of the Paris Commune for burning buildings including the Tuileries palace. The mother assumes that the picture, in which the "sparks look pretty in the wind," attracts the boy because of the fire, and she lightly replies (though with some irony) to his wanting to burn a palace, "But they had guns in France, and Christian men/Shot wicked little Communists, like you." When the boy insists he would have burned it anyway, innocently raising the question of the economic injustice it implied, the mother is forced to examine her own "soul." The rest of the poem deals with the bravery and cowardice introduced in the first stanza. Though "sweet" in appearance, the narrator knows the "stinging poison" and "shadowy power" she carries inside, seen in the image of the snake. Yet, the mother doubts she would ever have the courage to fully release the "utter life," the "unappealing, beautiful despair" of her darker nature, and so she is thus shamed by the palace-burner, this "being finer than my soul, I fear." Other examples of Piatt's skill with the dramatic monologue are "No Help," "Giving Back the Flower," "Mock Diamonds," "Carrigaline Castle," "Her Word of Reproach," and with a lighter touch, "Comfort through a Window," "Caprice at Home," "Story of a Storm," "A Pique at Parting," "His Argument," and "After Her First Party."

Piatt is not afraid of exploring paradoxical truths or of the complexity of her own feelings. Because the tensions and contradictions in her own life never permitted her to see the world from a single point of view, she had to develop other strategies to convey multiple levels of meaning in her poetry. Bennett writes that "Piatt, to a degree unmatched by any other poet with whom I am familiar, relies on dialogue (and on 'hints, and innuendoes, and questions [she] neglects to answer'), when writing." She avoids simple closure, often leaving the reader with no concrete conclusion except a sense of the ambiguity that reflects real life. The refusal to supply historical or autobiographical background, or the unannounced movement through different time-frames in some poems forces the reader to experience the moment of the poem and its immediate meaning. The dramatic structure of so many poems also allows her to deal with complex themes indirectly, and thus avoid sounding didactic, while at the same time letting her employ greater irony and other subtle nuances of style and voice.

She also uses symbolism in a complex, but usually consistent way. Many poems rely on an intricate system of symbols (flowers of all types in all states of bloom, jewels and gems, aspects of the crescent moon, gradations of light/dark and dry/wet and hot/cold, colors, music/silence, and dozens more), which she uses not merely for poetic effect but to enrich her subject and make it universal. The rose is probably her most common symbol, especially in the Civil War era poems, but she also imbues the snake, the desert, the South, angels, fairies, and other symbols with fine shades of meaning. She is even capable of poking fun at traditional Victorian symbols, like the dove or the saint in poems such as "A Pique at Parting," by using them in unexpected ways.

Because her poetry is often dark, angry, and complex, with sharp images and rough meters, she was not as popular in her own day as more conventional and "graceful" poets. She was criticized for being too "original," and for her Donne-like "abrupt" shifts of thought or mood. Her directness, dramatic sense, and sometimes bitter irony did not always keep her within the bounds of what was expected from a good "poetess." Although some critics found her originality refreshing, others tempered their comments like the reviewer in <u>The Scotsman</u>, an Edinburgh journal, (January 1, 1886):

> There is a fugitive beauty, a magical suggestiveness about her poems that are seen to best advantage in the shorter pieces; in the longer poems the mind grows a little weary of an everlasting steeplechase after shadowy thoughts and fleeting fancies, through labyrinths of parentheses and over a long and bristling series of dashes and pauses.

Not many of her contemporary readers, who were used to more easily-accessible poems, were willing to make the effort her poetry required, especially those readers put off by her blunt honesty and angry iconoclasm. Poems like "Giving Back the Flower," "A Hundred Years Ago," "The Grave at Frankfort," " A Mistake in the Bird-Market," "Mock Diamonds," were never collected into her books, and many others that did appear in her published volumes must have struck her late-Victorian readers as appallingly harsh and difficult. Yet she was also capable of delightful humor, childlike simplicity, playful exchanges, and even lyric grace. Perhaps her most beautiful poem, "A Daffodil," written in her seventies, shows how complete was her poetic gift.

It has been well over a hundred years since Sarah Piatt last published a book of new poems. Yet, as with Emily Dickinson, her originality and complexity may be more appreciated by modern readers than by her own generation. Bennett compares her in some ways with Ibsen, and adds: "Although her broken style and rough meters helped prepare the public ear for Dickinson, and her urban settings, use of fragmentary dialogues, and ironic, even cynical, perspective helped prepare the way for modernists such as T.S. Eliot, she herself was forgotten." There can be no doubt, however, that she created a body of exceptional work, a number of poems which will perhaps speak more powerfully to a new generation of readers ready to enter the new world of her poetry.

History of Piatt's Publications

The Nests at Washington was published in 1864, an anonymous collection of forty-four poems by John James Piatt followed by twenty-two of Sarah's poems. Her first individually published book was titled A Woman's Poems (1871), which incorporated eighteen of the poems from Nests along with many new ones that include some of her best work. During the 1870s, volumes of her poems appeared in rapid succession. A Voyage to the Fortunate Isles (1874) and That New World and Other Poems (1877) are both large collections of new poems. Poems in Company with Children (a collection) appeared in 1877 followed by more of her best original work in Dramatic Persons and Moods in 1880. As her reputation grew, she was published more frequently in major magazines, with nine poems published in 1876 and thirteen more the following year. In all, over one hundred of her poems appeared in widely-circulated periodicals like The Atlantic (twenty-seven times by Bennett's count), Scribner's, Harper's, Appleton's Journal, Century, Independent, Galaxy, Lippincott's, and Cosmopolitan.

Her books, even if not as popular as those of some other women poets, received mostly favorable reviews. The St. James Gazette commented in 1885, "There is so much room in our literature for verse which is playful without being exactly humorous, that it is to be hoped Mrs. Piatt will pursue further a vein in which she is so eminently successful." Other critics praised her "distinct and pleasing originality," her "taste," and her "dramatic instinct which helps so greatly to make a poem intense and vivid." Her poems were described by other reviewers as having a "solid kernel of fresh, original thought in each of them," "careful and conscientious artistry," "peculiar charm," and even "deep-hearted suggestiveness." One writer called her poetry "charmingly sincere," "artless," "piquant," "full of quaint surprise," and "racy"--all in the same review (in The Saturday Review, March 13, 1886).

Piatt's poems with children found special favor with her critics. A London reviewer in 1886 refers to "her wonderful, and, as it would seem, intuitive power of analysing child-nature." Another reviewer in Dublin states: "In her description of children and their ways Mrs. Piatt could not be surpassed for accuracy...her whole heart goes out to them, as she watches their movements with the deep interest of her loving, sympathetic nature." The review goes on to praise "these extraordinary and, with all their sadness, really beautiful poems." Edmund Stedman added, "She has a special gift of seeing into a child's heart."

During her years in Ireland (1882-1893) when her husband was United States Consul at Cork, Piatt became acquainted with other literary figures such as Edmund Gosse, Lady Wilde, Alice Meynell, Austin Dobson, Edmund Dowden, Katharine Tynan, and William Butler Yeats, and she and her husband are mentioned in various letters and memoirs of the time. British critics often compared her with Elizabeth Barrett Browning and Christina Rossetti (a favorite poet of her husband's). For example, The Saturday Review of London (July 11, 1885) declares that "one poem ['The Gift of Tears'--certainly not among her best] might have proceeded from Mrs. Browning. The kinship we claim for it is no light thing, and it is not lightly claimed."

Perhaps the most gratifying praise came from no less than William Butler Yeats in an unsigned review of An Enchanted Castle in the London Speaker (July 22, 1893). The Piatts knew Yeats slightly, and their daughter Marian once attended the theater with him to see his "The Land of Heart's Desire." In the review Yeats turns "with pleasure" from the three other writers he is discussing "to one who has a pure aesthetic ideal, and is a master of her sphere." He quotes in full one of the poems that deals with children, "In the Round Tower at Cloyne," and says that it is "surely perfect after its kind." Her poems from Ireland were published in An Irish Garland (1885), In Primrose Time (1886), An Irish Wild-Flower (1891), and collected in An Enchanted Castle (1893).

Yet, soon after her Poems (1894) was published in two volumes in London, her books all slipped out of print. As the new century arrived with Sarah and her husband back in Cincinnati, her work gradually passed from public notice, and by the time of her death it had almost completely disappeared from view. Eleven poems had appeared in Stedman's landmark An American

Anthology (1900) and twenty-one poems were printed in Emerson Venable's locally important Poets of Ohio (1909), but except for one poem each in anthologies by Rittenhouse (1915), Kilmer (1917), and LeGallienne (1925), Piatt received no mention in any other major anthology until almost the end of the twentieth century, and only occasional inclusion in a few minor ones. Even Walker's thorough American Women Poets of the Nineteenth Century (1992) does not include any of her poems.

Finally, in 1993, John Hollander included "Giving Back the Flower" in his two-volume American Poetry: The Nineteenth Century, and recently a few scholars, largely through Bennett's influence, have begun to take notice of Piatt's work. Karen Kilcup, after Bennett provided her with copies of Piatt's poetry, included fourteen poems in her 1997 anthology, Nineteenth-Century American Women Writers, published the same year as Janet Gray's She Wields a Pen: American Women Poets of the Nineteenth Century, which included three of Piatt's poems. In 1998, Bennett printed twenty-four more poems in her own Nineteenth-Century American Women Poets anthology, and will soon bring out a major collection of Piatt's poetry.

* * *

The poems selected for this volume have been arranged chronologically as they appeared in Sarah Piatt's book publications, along with a number of poems in the final section that were published only in periodicals. The date of first publication in a periodical or otherwise the first book publication is given at the end of each poem. Poems were chosen on the general aesthetic principle of how well they accomplish what they set out to do. Yet, with Piatt, some very ambitious poems, even if flawed, deserve to be included in any compilation of her best work. Although it is a temptation to select only the poems that are most successful and rewarding, it is also necessary to represent the rich variety of her work. For that reason, darker poems like "Beatrice Cenci," "The Descent of the Angel," "A New Thanksgiving," "Shapes of a Soul," "The Grave at Frank-fort," or John Hollander's excellent choice for a modern anthology, "Giving Back the Flower," appear alongside lighter, more anthologized poems such as "A Word with a Skylark," "Asking for Tears," "After Wings," and "Questions of the Hour."

No selection of Piatt's work would be representative without including examples from the many aspects of her life and career. Poems that deal with slavery, the Civil War, the South, the frustrations of her marriage, the tragic death of her children, beggars, her own inner conflicts, the loss of innocence and youth, her years in Ireland, her reading of history, faith and doubt, wealth and poverty, and her approaching old age are all represented in this selection. Also, poems have been chosen to show Piatt's versatility of tone and style, with examples of her use of irony, broad humor, self-mockery, playful conversation, dramatic monologue, biting cynicism, brutal honesty, wistfulness, and gentle lyricism. The four major volumes published between 1871 and 1880 include much of her best work and are thus amply represented here, although some of the poems written in Ireland are of the same quality and many of them are of historical interest as well. The uncollected poems in the last section include some of the most powerful Piatt ever wrote.

The text of the poems has been taken from their first appearance in Piatt's published books, except when only periodical publication is available. No changes to the original texts have been made, except in a few instances where double punctuation has been simplified or hyphens eliminated from "to-day" or "to-morrow."

*

PIATT'S DEDICATION:

(From <u>A Woman's Poems</u>, 1871)

- * -

TO

MY NEAREST NEIGHBOR

LOVED AS MYSELF--AND MORE!

THIS BOOK IS YOURS, NOT MINE, TO GIVE OR TAKE.

YOUR HAND, NOT MINE, HAS SENT IT FROM YOUR DOOR.

MY HEART GOES WITH IT--ONLY FOR YOUR SAKE.

MY GHOST

(A Story Told To My Little Cousin Kate)

Yes, Katie, I think you are very sweet,
  Now that the tangles are out of your hair,
And you sing as well as the birds you meet,
  That are playing, like you, in the blossoms there.
But now you are coming to kiss me, you say:
  Well, what is it for? Shall I tie your shoe,
Or loop your sleeve in a prettier way?
  "Do I know about ghosts?" Indeed I do.

"Have I seen one?" Yes: last evening, you know,
  We were taking a walk that you had to miss,
(I think you were naughty and cried to go,
  But, surely, you'll stay at home after this!)
And, away in the twilight lonesomely
  ("What is the twilight?" It's--getting late!)
I was thinking of things that were sad to me--
  There, hush! you know nothing about them, Kate.

Well, we had to go through the rocky lane,
  Close to that bridge where the water roars,
By a still, red house, where the dark and rain
  Go in when they will at the open doors;
And the moon, that had just waked up, looked through
  The broken old windows and seemed afraid,
And the wild bats flew and the thistles grew
  Where once in the roses the children played.

Just across the road by the cherry-trees
  Some fallen white stones had been lying so long,
Half hid in the grass, and under these
  There were people dead. I could hear the song
Of a very sleepy dove, as I passed
  The graveyard near, and the cricket that cried;

And I looked (ah! the Ghost is coming at last!)
  And something was walking at my side.

It seemed to be wrapped in a great dark shawl,
  (For the night was a little cold, you know.)
It would not speak. It was black and tall;
  And it walked so proudly and very slow.
Then it mocked me--everything I could do:
  Now it caught at the lightning-flies like me;
Now it stopped where the elder-blossoms grew;
  Now it tore the thorns from a gray bent tree.

Still it followed me under the yellow moon,
  Looking back to the graveyard now and then,
Where the winds were playing the night a tune--
  But, Katie, a Ghost doesn't care for <u>men</u>,
And your papa <u>couldn't</u> have done it harm!
  Ah, dark-eyed darling, what is it you see?
There, you needn't hide in your dimpled arm--
  It was only my Shadow that walked with me!

1864

GASLIGHT AND STARLIGHT

Those flowers of flame that blossom at night
　　From the dust of the city, along the street,
And wreathe rich rooms with their leaves of light,
　　Were dropping their tremulous bloom at my feet.

And the men whose names by the crowd are known,
　　And the women uplifted to share their place--
Some of them bright with their jewels alone,
　　Some of them brighter with beauty and grace--

Were around me under the flashing rays,
　　All seeming, I thought, as I saw them there,
To ask the throng, in their pleased, mute ways,
　　For its bow, or its smile, or at least its stare.

But, faint with the odors that floated about,
　　And tired of the glory the few can win,
I turned to the window: the darkness without
　　Struck heavily on the glitter within,

Still the glare behind me haunted my brain,
　　And I thought: "They are blest who are shining so;"
But a voice replied: "You are blinded and vain--
　　Such triumph when highest is often low.

"For some," it said, with a slow, sad laugh,
　　Who wear so proudly their little names,
Have leant on the People, as on a staff
　　To help them up to their selfish fames.

"And others yet--it is hard to know--
　　Have crawl'd through the dust to their sunny hour,
To crawl the same in its warmth and glow
　　And hiss the snake in the colors of Power.

"Yet it is comfort to feel, through the whole,
    They only look great, in God's calm eyes,
Who lean on the still, grand strength of the soul
    And climb toward the pure, high light of the skies."

1864

MY WEDDING RING

My heart stirr'd with its golden thrill
  And flutter'd closer up to thine,
In that blue morning of the June
  When first it clasp'd thy love and mine.

In it I see the little room,
  Rose-dim and hush'd with lilies still,
Where the old silence of my life
  Turn'd into music with "I will."

Oh, I would have my folded hands
  Take it into the dust with me:
All other little things of mine
  I'd leave in the bright world with thee.

1864

TO MARIAN ASLEEP

The full moon glimmers still and white,
  Where yonder shadowy clouds unfold;
The stars, like children of the Night,
  Lie with their little heads of gold
On her dark lap: nor less divine,
And brighter, seems your own and mine.

My darling, with your snowy sleep
  Folded around your dimpled form,
Your little breathings calm and deep,
  Your mother's arms and heart are warm;
You wear as lilies in your breast
The dreams that blossom from your rest.

Ah, must your clear eyes see ere long
  The mist and wreck on sea and land,
And that old haunter of all song,
  The mirage hiding in the sand?
And will the dead leaves in the frost

Tell you of song and summer lost?
And shall you hear the ghastly tales
  From the slow, solemn lips of Time--
Of Wrong that wins, of Right that fails,
  Of trampled Want and gorgeous Crime,
Of Splendor's glare in lighted rooms
And Famine's moan in outer glooms?

Of armies in their red eclipse
  That mingle on the smoking plain;
Of storms that dash our mighty ships
  With silks and spices through the main;
Of what it costs to climb or fall--
Of Death's great Shadow ending all?

But, baby Marian, do I string
  The dark with darker rhymes for you,
Forgetting that you came in Spring,
  The child of sun and bloom and dew,
And that I kiss'd, still fresh today,
The rosiest bud of last year's May?

Forgive me, pretty one: I know,
  Whatever sufferings onward lie,
Christ wore his crown of thorns below
  To gain his crown of light on high;
And when the lamp's frail flame is gone,
Look up: the stars will still shine on.

1864

43

HEARING THE BATTLE--July 21, 1861

One day in the dreamy summer,
  On the Sabbath hills, from afar
We heard the solemn echoes
  Of the first fierce words of war.

Ah, tell me, thou veiled Watcher
  Of the storm and the calm to come,
How long by the sun or shadow
  Till these noises again are dumb.

And soon in a hush and glimmer
  We thought of the dark, strange fight,
Whose close in a ghastly quiet
  Lay dim in the beautiful night.

Then we talk'd of coldness and pallor,
  And of things with blinded eyes
That stared at the golden stillness
  Of the moon in those lighted skies;

And of souls, at morning wrestling
  In the dust with passion and moan,
So far away at evening
  In the silence of worlds unknown.

But a delicate wind beside us
  Was rustling the dusky hours,
As it gather'd the dewy odors
  Of the snowy jessamine-flowers.

And I gave you a spray of the blossoms,
  And said: "I shall never know
How the hearts in the land are breaking,
  My dearest, unless you go."

1864

44

THE FANCY BALL

As Morning you'd have me rise
  On that shining world of art;
You forget: I have too much dark in my eyes--
  And too much dark in my heart.

"Then go as the Night--in June:
  Pass, dreamily, by the crowd,
With jewels to mock the stars and the moon,
  And shadowy robes like cloud.

"Or as Spring, with a spray in your hair
  Of blossoms as yet unblown;
It will suit you well, for our youth should wear
  The bloom in the bud alone.

"Or drift from the outer gloom
  With the soft white silence of Snow:"
I should melt myself with the warm, close room--
  Or my own life's burning. No.

"Then fly through the glitter and mirth
  As a Bird of Paradise:"
Nay, the waters I drink have touch'd the earth;
  I breathe no summer of spice.

"Then---" Hush: if I go at all,
  (It will make them stare and shrink,
It will look so strange at a Fancy Ball),
  I will go as--Myself, I think!

1866

45

AFTER WINGS

This was your butterfly, you see--
  His fine wings made him vain:
The caterpillars crawl, but he
  Passed them in rich disdain. --
My pretty boy says, "Let him be
  Only a worm again!"

O child, when things have learned to wear
  Wings once, they must be fain
To keep them always high and fair:
  Think of the creeping pain
Which even a butterfly must bear
  To be a worm again!

1871

MY BABES IN THE WOOD

I know a story, fairer, dimmer, sadder,
  Than any story painted in your books.
You are so glad? It will not make you gladder;
  Yet listen, with your pretty restless looks.

"Is it a Fairy Story?" Well, half fairy--
  At least it dates far back as fairies do,
And seems to me as beautiful and airy;
  Yet half, perhaps the fairy half, is true.

You had a baby sister and a brother,
  (Two very dainty people, rosily white,
Each sweeter than all things except the other!)
  Older yet younger--gone from human sight!

And I, who loved them, and shall love them ever,
  And think with yearning tears how each light hand
Crept toward bright bloom or berries--I shall never
  Know how I lost them. Do you understand?

Poor slightly golden heads! I think I missed them
  First, in some dreamy, piteous, doubtful way;
But when and where with lingering lips I kissed them,
  My gradual parting, I can never say.

Sometimes I fancy that they may have perished
  In shadowy quiet of wet rocks and moss,
Near paths whose very pebbles I have cherished,
  For their small sakes, since my most lovely loss.

I fancy, too, that they were softly covered
  By robins, out of apple-flowers they knew,
Whose nursing wings in far home sunshine hovered,
  Before the timid world had dropped the dew.

Their names were--what yours are! At this you wonder.
  Their pictures are--your own, as you have seen;
And my bird-buried darlings, hidden under
  Lost leaves--why, it is your dead selves I mean!

1870

SHAPES OF A SOUL

White with the starlight folded in its wings,
And nestling timidly against your love,
For this soft time of hushed and glimmering things,
You call my soul a dove, a snowy dove.

If I shall ask you in some shining hour,
When bees and odors through the clear air pass,
You'll say my soul buds as a small flush'd flower,
Far off, half hiding, in the old home-grass.

Ah, pretty names for pretty moods; and you,
Who love me, such sweet shapes as these can see;
But, take it from its sphere of bloom and dew,
And where will then your bird or blossom be?

Could you but see it, by life's torrid light,
Crouch in its sands and glare with fire-red wrath,
My soul would seem a tiger, fierce and bright
Among the trembling passions in its path.

And, could you sometimes watch it coil and slide,
And drag its colors through the dust a while,
And hiss its poison under foot, and hide,
My soul would seem a snake-- ah, do not smile!

Yet fiercer forms and viler it can wear;
No matter, though, when these are of the Past,
If as a Lamb in the Good Shepherd's care
By the still waters it lie down at last.

1867

49

DEATH BEFORE DEATH

Are mine the empty eyes
That stare toward the little new grave on the beautiful
burial-hill?
Was mine the last wet kiss that lies
Shut up in his coffin, kissing him still,
Kissing him still?

Is mine the hollow room?
Was it not cruel to take all the pretty small furniture,
say?--
The fairy pictures and heaps of bloom,
And music of mock-harps--so far away,
So far away?

Is mine the hidden face
That one night's sudden dread watching has thinn'd
and faded so much?--
Mine the lonesome hands through bitter space,
Yearning for something they never can touch,
Never can touch?

Is mine the passionate pain
That will hearken the trembling wind and feel the wide
still snow,
And sob at night with the sobbing rain,
And only feel that I can not know,
I can not know?

Was mine that lovely child?
Did he drop from my heart and go where the Powers
of the dust can destroy?
Can I see the very way he smiled---
"Let God keep his angels"? Do I want my boy--
I want my boy?

Is he gone from his air,
From his sun, from his voice, his motion, his mother,
                    his world, and his skies,
    From the unshorn light in his sweet hair,
From the elusion of his butterflies,
                              His butterflies?

    If not, why let me go
Where another sorrow is watching a small, cold bed
                    alone,
    And whisper how I have loved her so,
That to save her darling I gave my own,
                              I gave my own!

    Ah! if I learn'd her part,
And my dark fancies but play'd in despair like tragedy
                    queens,
    Then my only audience was my heart,
And my tears, that <u>were</u> tears, were behind the scenes,
                              Behind the scenes.

                              1871

OFFERS FOR THE CHILD

In the dim spaces of a dream, you see--
  Somewhere, perhaps, or else not anywhere,
(Remember in a dream what things may be)--
  I met a stranger with the whitest hair.

From his wide, wandering beard the snow-flakes whirl'd--
  (His face when young, no doubt, was much admired):
His name was Atlas, and he held the world;
  I held a child--and both of us were tired.

"A handsome boy," he courteously said;
  "He pleases my old fancy. What fine eyes!"
"Yes, father, but he wearies me. My head
  Is aching, too, and--listen how he cries!"

"If you would let me take him" --and he spread
  All his fair laces and deep velvets wide;
Then hid them from my smile, and, in their stead,
  Sweet jewels and vague sums of gold he tried.

Then ships, all heavy with the scents and sounds
  Of many a sea, the stains of many a sun;
Then palaces, with empires for their grounds,
  Were slowly offer'd to me, one by one.

"Then take the world! It will amuse you. So,
  Watch while I move its wires." An instant, then,
He laugh'd. "Look, child, at his quick puppet-show:"
  I saw a rich land dusk with marching men.

"This puppet, with the smile inscrutable,
  You call The Emperor; these, Statesmen; these--
No matter; this, who just now plays the fool,
  Is"--- "Not our"--- "It is, madam, if you please!"

"Hush!---" "Take the world and move them as you will!--
  Give me the boy." ---Then, shivering with affright,
I held the close cheek's dimples closer still,
  And bade the old Peddler--for I woke--good-night!

                                        1871

EARTH IN HEAVEN

Somewhere, my friend, in the beautiful skies,
    Awaiting us lovely and clear,
We shall find all beauty that leaves our eyes
    So vacant in vanishing here:
Not the human alone has died
To go up and be glorified.

I shall find my childhood playing there
    In the grass where it used to play,
And see our red-birds brighten the air;
    Again as a girl I shall stray
On the hills where the snow-drops grew,
And hear the wild doves in the dew.

I shall feel the darkness dripping with rain
    On the old home-roof; I shall see
The white rose-bud in the yard again,
    And the sweet-brier climbing the tree,
With its pretty young blooms that fell
Below to be drown'd in the well.

And sometimes a night, with blossoming hours
    In a crescent's early gleam,
Will let a Dream flutter out of its flowers,
    With no other name but a Dream,
To my breast, with a timid grace
And wings o'er its blushing face.

Ah! you smile in the dark; you smile, and refuse
    My faith in these sweet faded things;
But I tell you I know that my soul would lose
    One-half of the strength in its wings
If these were not keeping their light,
As the angels in Heaven, tonight.

1871

HER LAST GIFT

Come here. I know while it was May
   My mouth was your most precious rose,
My eyes your violets, as you say.
   Fair words, as old as Love, are those.

I gave my flowers while they were sweet,
   And sweetly you have kept them, all
Through my slow Summer's great last heat
   Into the lonely mist of Fall.

Once more I give them. Put them by,
   Back in your memory's faded years--
Yet look at them, sometimes; and try,
   Sometimes, to kiss them through your tears.

I've dimly known, afraid to know,
   That you should have new flowers to wear;
Well, buds of rose and violets blow
   Before you in the unfolding air.

So take from other hands, I pray,
   Such gifts of flowers as mine once gave:
I go into the dust, since they
   Can only blossom from my grave.

1871

A CHILD'S FIRST SIGHT OF SNOW

Oh, come and look at his blue, sweet eyes,
    As, through the window, they glance around
And see the glittering white surprise
    The Night has laid on the ground!

This beautiful Mystery you have seen,
    So new to your life, and to mine so old,
Little wordless Questioner---"What does it mean?"
    Why, it means, I fear, that the world is cold.

1870

QUESTIONS OF THE HOUR

"Do angels wear white dresses, say?
    Always, or only in the summer? Do
Their birthdays have to come like mine, in May?
    Do they have scarlet sashes then, or blue?

"When little Jessie died last night,
    How could she walk to Heaven--it is so far?
How did she find the way without a light?
    There wasn't even any moon or star.

"Will she have red or golden wings?
    Then will she have to be a bird, and fly?
Do they take men like presidents and kings
    In hearses with black plumes clear to the sky?

"How old is God? Has he gray hair?
    Can he see yet? Where did he have to stay
Before--you know--he had made--Anywhere?
    Who does he pray to--when he has to pray?

"How many drops are in the sea?
    How many stars? --well, then, you ought to know
How many flowers are on an apple-tree?
    How does the wind look when it doesn't blow?

"Where does the rainbow end? And why
    Did--Captain Kidd--bury the gold there? When
Will this world burn? And will the firemen try
    To put the fire out with the engines then?

"If you should ever die, may we
    Have pumpkins growing in the garden, so
My fairy godmother can come for me,
    When there's a prince's ball, and let me go?

"Read Cinderella just once more--
    What makes--men's other wives--so mean?" I know
That I was tired, it may be cross, before
    I shut the painted book for her to go.

Hours later, from a child's white bed
    I heard the timid, last queer question start:
"Mamma, are you--my stepmother?" it said.
    The innocent reproof crept to my heart.

                        1871

TALK ABOUT GHOSTS

(At Bed-Time)

"Each of us carries within him a future ghost."

What is a ghost? "It is something white,
(And I guess it goes barefooted, too,)
That comes from the graveyard in the night,
When the doors are lock'd, and breaks right through."
What does it do?

"Oh, it frightens people ever so much,
And goes away when the chickens crow;
And--doesn't steal any spoons, or touch
One thing that isn't its own, you know."
Who told you so?

"Somebody--every body, almost;
Or I knew, myself, when this world begun.
Not even a General could kill a ghost---
I wish the Lord had never made one.
They hate the sun!"

No, sweetest of all wee brown-eyed girls,
They love the light--'tis the dark they fear;
Love riches and power, love laces and pearls;
Love--all the preacher calls vanity here.
This much is clear.

"Do they love to be dead?" I can but tell
That few of them greatly love to die:
Perhaps they doubt whether all is well
In the place where ghosts--yes, "up in the sky."
You wonder why?

They love their clothes (and want to keep dress'd:)
Whether new and prettily white and red,
Or gray and ragged, 'tis hard, at best,
To take them off--though the prayers are said--
And go to bed.

1871

PLAYING BEGGARS

"Let us pretend we are two beggars." "No,
    For beggars are im---- something, something bad;
You <u>know</u> they are, because Papa says so,
    And Papa when he calls them that looks mad;
You should have seen him, how he frown'd one day,
When Mamma gave his wedding-coat away."

"Well, now he can't get married any more,
    Because he has no wedding-coat to wear.
But that poor ragged soldier at the door
    Was starved to death in prison once somewhere,
And shot dead somewhere else, and it was right
To give him coats--because he had to fight.

"Now let's be beggars." "They're im--posters. Yes,
    That's what they are, im--posters; and that means
Rich people, for they all <u>are</u> rich, I guess--
    Richer than we are, rich as Jews or queens,
And <u>they're</u> just playing beggars when they cry---"
"Then let us play like they do, you and I."

"Well, we'll be rich and wear old naughty clothes."
    "But they're <u>not</u> rich. If they were rich they'd buy
All the fine horses at the fairs and shows
    To give to General Grant. I'll <u>tell</u> you why:
Once when the rebels wanted to kill all
The men in this <u>world</u>--<u>he</u> let Richmond fall!

"<u>That</u> broke them up! I like the rebels, though,
    Because they have the curliest kind of hair.
One time, so many years and years ago,
    I saw one over in Kentucky there.
It show'd me such a shabby sword and said
It wanted to cut off--Somebody's head!

"But--<u>do</u> play beggar. You be one; and, mind,
    Shut up one eye, and get all over dust,
And say this: 'Lady, be so very kind
    As to give me some water. Well, I must
Rest on your step, I think, ma'am, for a while---
I've walk'd full twenty if I've walk'd one mile.

"'Lady, this is your little girl, I know:
    She is a beautiful child--and just like you;
You look too young to be her mother, though.
    This handsome boy is like his father, too:
The gentleman was he who pass'd this way
And look'd so cross?--so pleasant I <u>should</u> say.

"'But trouble, Lady, trouble puts me wrong.
    Lady, I'm sure you'll spare a dress or two--
You look so stylish. (Oh, if I was strong!)
    And shoes? Yours are too small. I need them new.
The money---thank you! Now you have some tea,
And flour, and sugar, you'll not miss, for me?

"'Ah, I forgot to tell you that my house
    Was burn'd last night. My baby has no bread,
And I'm as poor, ma'am, as a cellar-mouse.
    My husband died once; my grandmother's dead--
She was a good soul (but she's gone, that's true---
You have some coffee, madam?)--so are you.'"

"Oh, it's too long. I can't say half of <u>that</u>!
    I'll not be an im--poster, any how.
(But I should like to give one my torn hat,
    So I could get a prettier one, just now.)
They're worse than Christians, ghosts, or--any thing!
---I'll play that I'm a great man or a king."

1870

62

A PRESIDENT AT HOME

I pass'd a President's House today---
    "A President, mamma, and what is that?"
Oh, it is a man who has to stay
    Where bowing beggars hold out the hat
For something--a man who has to be
The Captain of every ship that we
Send with our darling flag to the sea--
The Colonel at home who has to command
Each marching regiment in the land.

This President now has a single room,
    That is low and not much lighted, I fear;
Yet the butterflies play in the sun and gloom
    Of his evergreen avenue, year by year;
And the child-like violets up the hill
Climb, faintly wayward, about him still;
And the bees blow by at the wind's wide will;
And the cruel river, that drowns men so,
Looks pretty enough in the shadows below.

Just one little fellow (named Robin) was there,
    In a red Spring vest, and he let me pass
With that charming-careless, high-bred air
    Which comes of serving the great. In the grass
He sat, half-singing, with nothing to do---
No, I did not see the President too:
His door was lock'd (what I say is true),
And he was asleep, and has been, it appears,
Like Rip Van Winkle, asleep for years!

1871

AN AFTER-POEM

You will read, or you will not read,
  That the lilies are whitest after they wither;
That the fairest buds stay shut in the seed,
  Though the bee in the dew say "Come you up hither."

You have seen, if you were not blind,
  That the moon can be crowded into a crescent,
And promise us light that we never can find
  When the midnights are wide and yellow and pleasant.

You will know, or you will not know,
  That the seas to the sun can fling their foam only,
And keep all their terrible waters below
  With the jewels and dead men quiet and lonely.

1871

ARMY OF OCCUPATION
(At Arlington, VA., 1866)

The summer blew its little drifts of sound--
  Tangled with wet leaf-shadows and the light
Small breath of scatter'd morning buds--around
The yellow path through which our footsteps wound.
  Below, the Capitol rose, glittering white,

There stretch'd a sleeping army. One by one,
  They took their places until thousands met;
No leader's stars flash'd on before, and none
Lean'd on his sword or stagger'd with his gun--
  I wonder if their feet have rested yet!

They saw the dust, they join'd the moving mass,
  They answer'd the fierce music's cry for blood,
Then straggled here and lay down in the grass:--
Wear flowers for such, shores whence their feet did pass;
  Sing tenderly, O river's haunted flood!

They had been sick, and worn, and weary, when
  They stopp'd on this calm hill beneath the trees:
Yet if, in some red-clouded dawn, again
The country should be calling to her men,
  Shall the reveille not remember these?

Around them underneath the mid-day skies
  The dreadful phantoms of the living walk,
And by low moons and darkness, with their cries--
The mothers, sisters, wives with faded eyes,
  Who call still names amid their broken talk.

And there is one who comes alone and stands
  At his dim fireless hearth--chill'd and oppress'd
By Something he has summon'd to his lands,
While the weird pallor of its many hands
  Points to his rusted sword in his own breast!

1866

65

THERE WAS A ROSE

"There was a Rose," she said,
  "Like other roses, perhaps, to you.
Nine years ago it was faint and red
  Away in the cold dark dew,
  On the dwarf bush where it grew.

"Never any rose before
  Was like that rose, very well I know;
Never another rose any more
  Will blow as that rose did blow,
  When the wet wind shook it so.

"'What do I want?'--Ah, what?
  Why, I want that rose, that wee one rose,
Only that rose. And that rose is not
  Anywhere just now? God knows
  Where all the old sweetness goes.

"I want that rose so much:
  I would take the world back there to the night
Where I saw it blush in the grass, to touch
  It once in that fair fall light,
  And only once, if I might.

"But a million marching men
  From the North and the South would arise?
And the dead--would have to die again?
  And the women's widowed cries
  Would trouble anew the skies?

"No matter. I would not care?
  Were it not better that this should be?
The sorrow of many, the many bear,--
  Mine is too heavy for me.
  And I want that rose, you see!"

1872

IF I WERE A QUEEN

"But if you were a Queen?" you said.
　Well, then I think my favorite page
Should have a yellow, restless head,
　And be just your own pretty age.
So sweet in violet velvet, he
　Should tend my butterflies in herds,
Or help that belted knight, the bee,
　Win honey, or make little birds
Some little songs to sing for me--
　　　　　　　　　If I were Queen.

A Queen--you saw one sitting by
　A tall man in a picture? Well.
He had a harp? You need not try--
　Her name is one you can not tell.
And so you wonder if I could
　Be Isolt, then? Not she, I fear,
To save Sir Tristram of the Wood
　And all his tripping silver deer;
For it were better to be good,
　　　　　　　　　If I were Queen.

Nor Guinevere--- You ask, would I
　Be Queen Elizabeth? Oh! no;
For, then, should I not have to die
　And leave, all hanging in a row,
Two thousand dresses? Could I bear
　To sit, majestic, cross, and gray,
With red paint on my nose, or wear,
　Down in my grave till Judgment Day,
The ring of Essex burning there,
　　　　　　　　　If I were Queen.

Now let me ask myself awhile.
　Mary of Scotland, then?--since she
Haunts her gray castle with a smile

That one man may have died to see:
She, fairest in Romance's light;
 She, saddest-storied of them all;
She--but it would not please me quite
 To climb a scaffold, or to fall
Beside my lovely head tonight,
                              If I were Queen.

Then she of Egypt--with the asp
 To drain my deadly beauty dry?--
To see my Roman lover clasp
 His sword with surer love, and die
Closer to it than me? Not so.
 No desert-snake with nursing grace
Should draw my fierce heart's fiercest glow;
 No coward of my conqueror's race
Should offer me his blood, I know--
                              If I were Queen.

Boadicea? I were afraid
 To see her scythed chariots shine!
---Nor Vashti; for she disobeyed
 Her lord, the king in kingly wine!
Then she, the Queen of the East, who found
 The Wisest not so well arrayed,
In all his glory, as the ground
 Arrays its lilies?--Would I fade
Into some shrunken Bible mound,
                              If I were Queen?

Semiramis? Were it not sweet
 To have a palace mirror show
How mad Assyria at my feet
 Might lie down like a lamb? And, oh!
To stand defiant, in the glare
 Of rising war, and softly say:
"My Beauty will subdue them!" Rare

And royal bloom must drop away;
Nor would I as a ghost look fair,
                    If I were Queen.

Penelope? No, on my word:
  Vexed grievously with suitors, while
Much-wandering Ulysses heard
  Fine singing at the syrens' isle,
Too small were Ithaca for me!
  Then she whose gold hair glitters high
With stars caught in its tangles? --See,
  How beautiful it is! But I
Should choose my hair on Earth to be,
                    If I were Queen!

Nor slight, blonde Marie Antoinette?
  Nor she the Austrians called their King?
Nor any Blanche, or Margaret?
  Nor Russia's Catharine? Would I bring
The Spanish woman's loath heart, then,
  From Aragon to England's throne?
Or be the Italian, widowed, when
  She, in a garret at Cologne,
Starved, a gray exile, shunned of men,
                    If I were Queen?

What Queen? Titania--since it seems
  A woman never quite can tire
Or kissing long, fair ears! In dreams
  My Gentle Joy I will admire,
And--but there is no Fairyland
  Left in the crowded world, no room
For dew, for any thing but sand.
  Put out the moonshine, fold the bloom.
My feet could find no space to stand,
                    If I were Queen.

Ah! still I ask myself what Queen?
   Well, one whose days were almost done,
Who felt her grave-grass turning green,
   Who saw the low light of the sun
Shrink from her palace windows, while
   Her whole court watched beside her bed,
Ready to say, without a smile:
   "We loved the Queen. The Queen is dead."
Then they should grieve a little while,
                    If I were Queen.

And my whole court, I think, should show
   Three little heads of lightest gold,
Two others of a darker glow;
   And One bent low enough to hold
Between pale, quivering hands. And then
   Some Silence should receive my soul,
My name should fade from lips of men,
   My pleasant funeral-bells should toll
This hour, and dust be dust again--
                    If I were Queen.

1874

THEIR TWO FORTUNES

(Annie, after Calling on Charlotte)

"As I passed her window she smiled at me,
  Through the lovely mist of her laces,
And asked if I would go in and see
  Those exquisite foreign vases.

"Then the mirrors here, or the bronzes there,
  Or some statue's cold completeness,
Or the flowers that followed her through the air,
  With their souls expressed in sweetness.

"From the carpets, full of their Eastern blooms,
  That were hiding her steps so lightly,
I passed to the love in my faded rooms,
  And my heart kept aching--slightly.

"If her life is dry, then its torrid sands
  Must have pained my eyes with their glitter,
For I know that I hid my face in my hands--
  And I fear that my tears were bitter.

"Ah, you pity her--because she is fair;
  And because--she wears rich dresses;
And because her lord has--not dark hair;
  And because of--certain guesses.

"But I tell you, sir, with your author's look,
  When the point of your pen grows tender
There are things as sad to put in your book
  As my lady's loveless splendor."

1871

71

THE ORDER FOR HER PORTRAIT

"I say what Cromwell said,
  (Smile, gray-haired skeptic, if you think me bold,)
And that Italian count whose hair was red--
  His great will would not have it painted gold.

"Look at me, if you will;
  Say youth is gone, or youth was never mine.
I change not with the seasons. Cold and still,
  I wait before you--careless and divine.

"Youth? Can the rose outstay
  The bud of the rose? And could the round moon shine
Without the crescent somewhere? Who shall say
  How far youth reaches? Not such voice is mine.

"No, I am brave, not vain;
  Braver than he of Macedon, since I
For Vanity's light sake would hardly stain
  Art and the awful future with a lie:

"You know that hand whose pride
  Within its hollow held one world, afar
Reaching for others, raised itself to hide
  On pictured brows the glory of a scar.

"But paint me as I am,
  Whatever shape or color you may see;
And do not fold the white fleece of the lamb
  About the yellow lioness, for me.

"Aye, as I am. And then,
  No matter what you on your canvas find,
It shall not shrink before the eyes of men;
  It shall be Truth--unless your soul be blind!"

1874

"I WANT IT YESTERDAY"

"Come, take the flower,--it is not dead,
   It stayed all night out in the dew."
"I will not have it now," he said;
   "I want it yesterday, I do."

"It is as red, it is as sweet"--
   With angry tears he turned away,
Then flung it fiercely at his feet,
   And said, "I want it--yesterday."

As sullen and as quick of grief,
   Sometimes a lovelier flower that this
I crush forever, scent and leaf;
   Then scent and leaf forever miss.

It keeps its blush, it keeps its breath,
   It keeps its form unchanged, but I
See in its beauty only death;
   Then drop it in the dust--and why?

And why? Ah, Hand divine, I know--
   Forgive my childish pain, I pray--
Today your flower is fair, but oh!
   I only want it--yesterday!

1874

MARBLE OR DUST?

A child, beside a statue, said to me,
  With pretty wisdom very sadly just,
"That man is Mr. Lincoln, mamma. He
  Was made of marble; we are made of dust."

One flash of passionate sorrow trembled through
  The dust of which I had been dimly made,
One fierce, quick wish to be of marble too--
  Not something meaner, that must fall and fade.

"To be forever fair and still and cold,"
  I faintly thought, with faint tears in my sight;
"To stand thus face to face with Time, and hold
  Between us that uncrumbling charm of white;

"To see the creatures formed of slighter stuff
  Waver in little dead-leaf whirls away,
Yet know that I could wait and have enough
  Of frost and dew, enough of dark and day.

"---I would be marble? Wherefore? Just to miss
  The tremors of glad pain that dust must know?--
The grief that settles after some dead kiss?--
  The frown that was a smile not long ago?

"Do I forget the stone's long loneliness?--
  The dumb impatience all wan watching brings?--
The looking with blind eyes, in vague distress,
  For Christ's slow Coming and the End of Things?

"No, boy of mine, with your young yellow hair,
  Better the dust you scatter with your feet
Than marble, which can see not you are fair--
  Than marble, which can feel not you are sweet.

"Ay, or than marble which must meet the years
　　Without my light relief of murmurous breath;
Without the bitter sweetness of my tears--
　　Without the love which dust must have for Death."

1871

SWEETNESS OF BITTERNESS

I wonder, if my hair were gray,
  It would not then be sweet to see
Some other head in gold, and say,
  Shaking my own: "Ah me! ah me!
  How very pleasant it must be
  To have such lovely hair as she!"

I wonder, if my days were shut,
  Empty and dim and slow with care,
In some poor peasant's prison-hut,
  It would not then be sweet to stare,
  With the fierce boldness of despair,
  Into some shining window, where

Each foreign flower, through lifted lace,
  Its passionate, homesick yearning shows,
On pictures warm with Southern grace
  Or cold with Northern birds and snows,
  And say: "How fair a fate have those
  Within whose world such beauty glows."

I wonder, if the broken breath
  Of one wet brier-rose held tonight
A little memory dear with death,
  It were not sweet to have the light
  Show laughing mothers full in sight
  Kiss dimpled things in baby-white.

I wonder, were I left alone,
  With asp and sun and sand, some day,
And circled with a fiery zone,
  'T would not be sweet to look away
  Toward lands where moonlit fountains play
  And toss to other lips their spray.

I wonder, were it mine to kiss
  A nun's black cross through tears, and wear
Her blinding veil, and miss and miss
  The world's one charm, if even there,
  High up in still and sacred air,
  Where thought itself is only prayer,

It would not then be sweet to make
  (And like a mateless bird to pine)
My wan and weary fingers ache
  With tracing some light leaf or vine
  In bridal drapery, faint and fine--
  Because it never could be mine!

I wonder, is there any thing
  In hidden honey half so sweet
As--something in the bee's wild sting;
  If buried wine, found at the feet
  Of some young king, were so complete
  As thirst within his fever's heat.

1874

BEATRICE CENCI

(Seen in a City Shop-Window)

Out of low light an exquisite faint face
    Suddenly started. Goldenness of hair,
A South-look of sweet-sorrowful eyes, a trace
    Of prison-paleness: what if these were there,
When Guido's hand could never reach the grace
    That glimmered on me from the Italian air--
    Fairness so fierce, or fierceness half so fair?

"Is it some Actress?" a slight school-boy said.
    Some Actress? Yes.
                        --The curtain rolled away,
Dusty and dim. The scene--among the dead--
    In some weird, gloomy-pillared palace lay;
The Tragedy, which we have brokenly read,
    With its two hundred ghastly years was gray:
    None dared applaud with flowers her shadowy way--
    Yet, ah! how bitterly well she seemed to play!

Hush! for a child's quick murmur breaks the charm
    Of terror that was winding round me so;
And, at the white touch of her pretty arm,
    Darkness and Death and Agony crouch low
In old-time dungeons: "Tell me, (is it harm
    To ask you?) is the picture real, though?--
    And why the beautiful ladies, all, you know,
    Live so far-off, and die so long ago?"

1871

78

OVER IN KENTUCKY

"This is the smokiest city in the world,"
  A slight voice, wise and weary, said, "I know.
My sash is tied, and, if my hair was curled,
  I'd like to have my prettiest hat and go
There where some violets had to stay, you said,
Before your torn-up butterflies were dead--
              Over in Kentucky."

Then one, whose half-sad face still wore the hue
  The North Star loved to light and linger on,
Before the war, looked slowly at me too,
  And darkly whispered: "What is gone is gone.
Yet, though it may be better to be free,
I'd rather have things as they used to be
              Over in Kentucky."

Perhaps I thought how fierce the master's hold,
  Spite of all armies, kept the slave within;
How iron chains, when broken, turned to gold,
  In empty cabins, where glad songs had been
Before the Southern sword knew blood and rust,
Before wild cavalry sprang from the dust,
              Over in Kentucky.

Perhaps---but, since two eyes, half-full of tears,
  Half-full of sleep, would love to keep awake
With fairy pictures from my fairy years,
  I have a phantom pencil that can make
Shadows of moons, far back and faint, to rise
On dewier grass and in diviner skies,
              Over in Kentucky.

For yonder river, wider than the sea,
  Seems sometimes in the dusk a visible moan
Between two worlds--one fair, one dear to me.

The fair has forms of ever-glimmering stone,
Weird-whispering ruin, graves where legends hide,
And lies in mist upon the charmed side,
                  Over in Kentucky.

The dear has restless, dimpled, pretty hands,
  Yearning toward unshaped steel, unfancied wars,
Unbuilded cities, and unbroken lands,
  With something sweeter than the faded stars
And dim, dead dews of my lost romance, found
In beauty that has vanished from the ground
                  Over in Kentucky.

1872

SAY THE SWEET WORDS

Say the sweet words, say them soon;
  You have said the bitter--
Changed to tears, by this dim moon
  You may see them glitter.

Say the sweet words soon, I pray--
  Mine is piteous pleading;
Haste to draw the steel away,
  Though the wound keep bleeding.

1874

LEAVING LOVE

"If one should stay in Italy awhile,
   With bloom to hide the dust beneath her feet,
With birds in love with roses to beguile
   Her life until its sadness grew too sweet.

"If she should, slowly, see some statue there,
   Divine with whiteness and with coldness, keep
A very halo in the hovering air;
   If she should weep--because it could not weep;

"If she should waste each early gift of grace
   In watching it with rapturous despair,
Should kiss her youth out on its stony face,
   And feel the grayness gathering toward her hair:

"Then fancy, though it had till now seemed blind,
   Blind to her little fairness, it could see
How scarred of soul, how wan and worn of mind,
   How faint of form and faded, she must be;

"If she should moan: 'Ah, land of flower and fruit,
   Ah, fiercely languid land, undo your charm!
Ah, song impassioned, make your music mute!
   Ah, bosom, shake away my clinging arm!'

"Then swiftly climb into the mountains near,
   And set her face forever toward the snow,
And feel the North in chasm and cliff, and hear
   No echo from the fairyland below;

"If she should feel her own new loneliness,
   With every deep-marked, freezing step she trod,
Nearing (and in its nearness growing less)
   The vast and utter loneliness of God;

"If back to scented valleys she should call,
This woman that I fancy--only she--
Would it remind one statue there at all,
O cruel Silence in the South, of--me?"

1874

THE BLACK PRINCESS

(A True Fable of my old Kentucky Nurse)

I knew a Princess: she was old,
  Crisp-haired, flat-featured, with a look
Such as no dainty pen of gold
  Would write of in a Fairy Book.

So bent she almost crouched, her face
  Was like the Sphinx's face, to me,
Touched with vast patience, desert grace,
  And lonesome, brooding mystery.

What wonder that a faith so strong
  As hers, so sorrowful, so still,
Should watch in bitter sands so long,
  Obedient to a burdening will!

This Princess was a Slave--like one
  I read of in a painted tale;
Yet free enough to see the sun,
  And all the flowers, without a veil.

Not of the Lamp, not of the Ring,
  The helpless, powerful Slave was she,
But of a subtler, fiercer Thing:
  She was the Slave of Slavery.

Court-lace nor jewels had she seen:
  She wore a precious smile, so rare
That at her side the whitest queen
  Were dark--her darkness was so fair.

Nothing of loveliest loveliness
  This strange, sad Princess seemed to lack;
Majestic with her calm distress
  She was, and beautiful though black:

Black, but enchanted black, and shut
  In some vague Giant's tower of air,
Built higher than her hope was. But
  The True Knight came and found her there.

The Knight of the Pale Horse, he laid
  His shadowy lance against the spell
That hid her Self: as if afraid,
  The cruel blackness shrank and fell.

Then, lifting slow her pleasant sleep,
  He took her with him through the night,
And swam a River cold and deep,
  And vanished up an awful Height.

And, in her Father's House beyond,
  They gave her beauty robe and crown:
---On me, I think, far, faint, and fond,
  Her eyes today look, yearning, down.

                    1872

THE FUNERAL OF A DOLL

They used to call her Little Nell,
  In memory of that lovely child
Whose story each had learned to tell.
  She, too, was slight and still and mild,
  Blue-eyed and sweet; she always smiled,
And never troubled any one
Until her pretty life was done.
And so they tolled a tiny bell,
  That made a wailing fine and faint,
As fairies ring, and all was well.
  Then she became a waxen saint.

Her funeral it was small and sad.
  Some birds sang bird-hymns in the air.
The humming-bee seemed hardly glad,
  Spite of the honey every-where.
  The very sunshine seem'd to wear
Some thought of death, caught in its gold,
That made it waver wan and cold.
Then, with what broken voice he had,
  The Preacher slowly murmured on
(With many warnings to the bad)
  The virtues of the Doll now gone.

A paper coffin rosily-lined
  Had Little Nell. There, drest in white,
With buds about her, she reclined,
  A very fair and piteous sight--
  Enough to make one sorry, quite.
And, when at last the lid was shut
Under white flowers, I fancied---but
No matter. When I heard the wind
  Scatter Spring-rain that night across
The Doll's wee grave, with tears half-blind
  One child's heart felt a grievous loss.

"It was a funeral, mamma. Oh,
   Poor Little Nell is dead, is dead.
How dark!--and do you hear it blow?
   She is afraid." And, and as she said
   These sobbing words, she laid her head
Between her hands and whispered: "Here
Her bed is made, the precious dear--
She can not sleep in it, I know.
   And there is no one left to wear
Her pretty clothes. Where did she go?
   --See, this poor ribbon tied her hair!"

                                    1872

CRYING FOR THE MOON

It is pretty because it is high;
  All things are pretty when out of reach,
And the prettiest things are kept in the sky.
Why? Can I ever tell you why?
God, I think, knows better than I.
  I shall have to learn what I can not teach.

But it is yellow sometimes, do you say,
  And sometimes red?--and you want it, too?
I wonder how long it would please your play.
Remember it does not shine by day,
And at night you'd have to put it away--
  You could not take it to bed with you.

Yes, but you can not have it, I fear--
  For a reason as good as we find in books:
For people as wise as you, and as queer,
Will cry for the moon, year after year,
And go to their graves without it, my dear:
  Because--it is larger than it looks!

1874

AUNT ANNIE

The old house has, for being sweet,
  Some sweeter reason than the rose
Which, red or white, about the feet
  Of many a nested home-bird grows.

And sadder reason than the rain
  On the quaint porch, for being sad,
(Oh, human pity, human pain!)
  The old house, in its shadows, had.

I sat within it as a guest,
  I who went from it as a wife;--
The young days there, though not the best,
  Had been the fairest of my life:

For love itself must ever seem
  More precious, to our restless youth,
When hovering subtly in its dream
  Than when we touch its nestling truth.

I sat there as a guest, I said--
  Holding the loveliest boy on earth,
With his fair, sleepy, yellow head
  Close to the pleasant shining hearth.

He laughed out in his sleep, and I
  Laughed too, and kissed him--when I heard
A wise and very cautious sigh;
  And once again the dimples stirred.

Aunt Annie looked at him awhile;
  Then shook her head at her own fears,
With more of sorrow in her smile
  Than I could ever put in tears.

"He _is_ a pretty boy I know--
    The prettiest in the world? Ah, me!
One other, fifty years ago,
    Was quite as pretty, dear, as he.

"Now I am eighty. Twenty-five
    Are gone since last we heard from James.
I sometimes think he is alive."
    She hushed, and looked into the flames.

"He used to tell me, when a child,
    Of far, strange countries, where they say
The flowers bloom all the year"--she smiled--
    "I can't believe it, to this day!

"And still I think he may have crossed
    The sea--and stayed the other side.
His letters may have all been lost--
    Who knows? Who knows? The world is wide.

"I often think, if you could know
    How much he makes me think of _him_,
You'd guess why I love Victor so."
    Again the troubled eyes were dim.

"If your child, such a night, were out
    Lost in this dark and snow and sleet,
You would go wild, I do not doubt."
    I almost heard her own heart beat.

"Yet long, on stormier nights than this,
    Mine has been out--why should I care
How many a winter now it is?
    Mine has been out--and God knows where."

                            1874

                   90

THE PALACE-BURNER

(A Picture in a Newspaper)

She has been burning palaces. "To see
  The sparks look pretty in the wind?" Well, yes--
And something more. But women brave as she
  Leave much for cowards, such as I, to guess.

But this is old, so old that everything
  Is ashes here--the woman and the rest.
Two years are--oh! so long. Now you may bring
  Some newer pictures. You like this one best?

You wish that you had lived in Paris then?--
  You would have loved to burn a palace, too?
But they had guns in France, and Christian men
  Shot wicked little Communists like you.

You would have burned the palace?--Just because
  You did not live in it yourself! Oh! why
Have I not taught you to respect the laws?
  You would have burned the palace--would not I?

Would I? Go to your play. Would I, indeed?
  I? Does the boy not know my soul to be
Languid and worldly, with a dainty need
  For light and music? Yet he questions me.

Can he have seen my soul more near than I?
  Ah! in the dusk and distance sweet she seems,
With lips to kiss away a baby's cry,
  Hands fit for flowers, and eyes for tears and dreams.

Can he have seen my soul? And could she wear
  Such utter life upon a dying face:
Such unappealing, beautiful despair:
  Such garments--soon to be a shroud--with grace?

Has she a charm so calm that it could breathe
  In damp, low places till some frightened hour;
Then start, like a fair, subtle snake, and wreathe
  A stinging poison with a shadowy power?

Would *I* burn palaces? The child has seen
  In this fierce creature of the Commune here,
So bright with bitterness and so serene,
  A being finer than my soul, I fear.

1872

"I WISH THAT I COULD GO"

They who look backward always look through tears.
   So, very dimly, somewhere, I do see
A door that opens into lonesome years,
   Furnished with--dust and silence! What can be
Sadder than absence of fair household sights,
Beloved pictures, warm and pleasant lights,
   In empty rooms where--- Does it call to me,
That first child-voice which taught my life to know
What music meant?--
               "I wish that I could go."

I turned and kissed her--"You had better stay."
   She heard the wood-bells ring among the herds:
"I want to see so many lambs today,"
   She answered in her little piteous words,
   Sweetly half-said and tenderly half-guessed;
"You said there was one robin with a nest
   Up in the apple-flowers. I love the birds--
Ever so many times--and you could show
Me where they sleep. I wish that I could go."

"It is too far. And here are butterflies;
   Look--one--two--three. Go, catch them if you will."
"I've seen all these too much--they hurt my eyes!
   They're naughty things--they never can be still!
I would not try to catch another one
Here, in the yard, to save its life! I'd run
   After some pretty new ones on the hill
Away off--almost to the skies! And, oh!
I'd be so sweet. I wish that I could go."

Nor was it only toward the clear white light,
   Led subtly on by many a violet,
She would have followed me. The great fierce Night
   Might lie beside our cottage, black and wet,
And make mad hungry noises. Still, if I

Thought fit to pass it, her appealing cry
   (The same that haunts me, sorrowfully, yet)
Was with me always--most forlorn and slow:
"If it is dark, I wish that I could go."

"If it is dark?"--what was the Dark? She knew.
   Just a brief bridge which others must have passed--
With a slight shiver, it might be--into
   A glitter of lamps: a life whose heart beat fast
Under sweet colors, jewels, music, all
The showers of fairy gifts that, fairily, fall
   On some Strange City, where----Oh! faint and vast
Time lies behind, yet nearer seems to grow
That eager sound:
                         "I wish that I could go."

It is in my own soul. Myself a child,
   Some ghostly doorway with my grief I fill;
Eager for blossoms beautiful and wild
   Just out of reach; eager to climb some hill,
So far away and almost to the skies,
And (tired of old ones) find new butterflies.
   Some One seems gone whom I would follow still.
Across the Dark I see your charmed glow,
Strange City, shine---
                         "I wish that I could go."

                                    1874

                                     94

THIS WORLD

Why do we love her?--that she gave us birth?
  How can we thank her for ourselves? Are we,
The pale, weak children of her old age, worth
  The light that shows--- there is a mirror. See!

Why do we love her? In her withering days,
  Careless or frozen-hearted, half-asleep,
She leaves us to our fierce and foolish plays,
  Nor kisses off the after-tears we weep.

She lets us follow our own childish cries,
  And find strange playmates; lets our baby hands
Reach for the red glare in the tiger's eyes,
  Or the fair snake--the rainbow of the sands.

She lets us climb, through deadly dews and vines,
  After illusive birds that nurse no song,
Or die for some faint wreath of snow, that shines
  On those great heights where gods alone belong.

Still let us love her for her lovely years.
  Yet beautiful with moonlight beauty, she
Now wonders vaguely, through forlornest tears,
  How far away her morning's sun may be.

Still let us love her. She is sad and blind,
  And with wan arms forever reaching back,
Into the dreadful dark of Space, to find
  Her radiant footsteps--that have left no track.

Still let us love her, though, indeed, she seems
  To give to our small wants small heed at best.
Let her sit muffled in her ancient dream,
  With souls of her first children at her breast.

Better she brood, with wide unshadowed eyes,
  On phantom Hebrews under phantom palms,
With phantom roses flushed, and phantom skies
  Brooding above them full of Bible calms;

Better she help the young Egyptian make
  His play-house pyramid with her fancy's hands,
Or teach his Memnon's pulseless heart to ache
  With hollow music in forgotten sands;

Better, in vanished temples, watch the Greek
  Carve his divine white toys; better she hold
The Roman's savage sword and hear the shriek,
  Than feel the silence through the silken fold;

For Antony's dusk queen to lift the snake,
  For Brutus' wife the shining death of fire--
Yea, all were better than to sit and take
  Dull honey from Today and never tire.

So let us love her, our poor Mother yet,
  For songs, for pictures that her sons have made;
Aye, let us love her more if she forget---
  To think of us would make her shrink, afraid!

1874

A MASKED BALL

There, in the music strangely met,
  From lands and ages wide apart,
They came, like ghosts remembering yet
  The old sweet yearning of the heart.

What sad and shining names were heard!
  What stories swept the dust, like trains!
What minster-buried echoes stirred!
  What backward splendors, backward stains!

Still two by two, as moved by fate,
  They came from silence and from song;
The tyranny of love or hate
  With that mock-pageant passed along.

There kings and cardinals long gone
  Forgot their feuds, and joined the dance.
His Holiness himself looked on,
  With something merry in his glance.

There, priestly, yet not loath to please,
  Stood Abelard; by some sad whim,
In convent coif, poor Heloise
  Was near, confessing--what?--to him.

There, with forlornest beauty wan,
  Young Amy Robsart walked unseen,
While my Lord Leicester's looks were on
  Elizabeth, his gracious queen.

There--though the blonde Rowena gazed,
  Gold-haired and stately, with surprise--
Jeweled and dark, Rebecca raised
  The Saxon knight half-wistful eyes.

And there, despite his inky cloak,
    The melancholy Dane seemed gay,
And to Polonius' daughter spoke
    Things Shakespeare does not have him say.

"I think," he said, "I know you by
    That most fantastic wreath you wear."
She, with a little languid sigh,
    Asked--if his father's ghost were there.

"That voice--though veiled, it can not hide.
    One trifling favor I would ask:
Give me--Yourself." "No, no," she cried;
    "You are--a stranger in a mask."

What more? Ah, well! Ophelia fled
    From Hamlet--when his mask was raised.
"I--was--mistaken," Hamlet said,
    As in Ophelia's face he gazed.

Ah, in the world, as at the ball,
    There is a mask that lovers wear;
We call it Youth. But let it fall,
    Then--Hamlet and Ophelia stare.

                              1874

                              98

A WOMAN'S BIRTHDAY

It is the Summer's great last heat,
It is the Fall's first chill: they meet.
Dust in the grass, dust in the air,
Dust in the grave--and every-where!
Ah, late rose, eaten to the heart:
Ah, bird, whose southward yearnings start:
The one may fall, the other fly.
Why may not I? Why may not I?

Oh, Life! that gave me for my dower
The hushing song, the worm-gnawed flower,
Let drop the rose from your shrunk breast
And blow the bird to some warm nest;
Flush out your dying colors fast:
The last dead leaf--will be the last.
No? Must I wear your piteous smile
A little while, a little while?

The withering world accepts her fate
Of mist and moaning, soon or late;
She had the dew, the scent, the spring
And upward rapture of the wing;
Their time is gone, and with it they.
And am I wooing Youth to stay
In these dry days, that still would be
Not fair to me, not fair to me?

If Time has stained with gold the hair,
Should he not gather grayness there?
Whatever gifts he chose to make,
If he has given, shall he not take?
His hollow hand has room for all
The beauty of the world to fall
Therein. I give my little part
With aching heart, with aching heart.

1874

99

THAT NEW WORLD

How gracious we are to grant to the dead
  Those wide, vague lands in the foreign sky,
Reserving this world for ourselves instead--
  For we must live, though others must die!

And what is this world that we keep, I pray?
  True, it has glimpses of dews and flowers;
Then Youth and Love are here and away,
  Like mated birds--but nothing is ours.

Ah, nothing indeed, but we cling to it all.
  It is nothing to hear one's own heart beat,
It is nothing to see one's own tears fall;
  Yet surely the breath of our life is sweet.

Yes, the breath of our life is so sweet, I fear
  We were loath to give it for all we know
Of that charmed Country we hold so dear,
  Far into whose beauty the breathless go.

Yet certain we are, when we see them fade
  Out of the pleasant light of the sun,
Of the sands of gold in the palm-leaf's shade,
  And the strange, high jewels all these have won.

You dare not doubt it, O soul of mine!
  And yet, if these empty eyes could see
One, only one, from that voyage divine,
  With something, anything, sure for me!

Ah, blow me the scent of one lily, to tell
  That it grew outside of this world, at most;
Ah, show me a plume to touch, or a shell
  That whispers of some unearthly coast!

1875

THE ALTAR AT ATHENS

"To the Unknown God"

Because my life was hollow with a pain
   As old as--death: because my eyes were dry
As the fierce tropics after months of rain:
   Because my restless voice said "Why?" and "Why?"

Wounded and worn, I knelt within the night,
   As blind as darkness-- Praying? And to Whom?--
When yon cold crescent cut my folded sight
   And showed a phantom Altar in my room.

It was the Altar Paul at Athens saw.
   The Greek bowed there, but not the Greek alone;
The ghosts of nations gathered, wan with awe,
   And laid their offerings on that shadowy stone.

The Egyptian worshiped there the crocodile,
   There they of Nineveh the bull with wings;
The Persian there, with swart sun-lifted smile,
   Felt in his soul the writhing fire's bright stings.

There the weird Druid held his mistletoe;
   There for the scorched son of the sand, coiled bright,
The torrid snake was hissing sharp and low;
   And there the Western savage paid his rite.

"Allah!" the Moslem darkly muttered there:
   "Brahma!" the jeweled Indies of the East
Sighed through their spices, with a languid prayer;
   "Christ?" faintly questioned many a paler priest.

And still the Athenian Altar's glimmering Doubt
   On all religions--evermore the same.
What tears shall wash its sad inscription out?
   What Hand shall write thereon His other name?

1877

LADY FRANKLIN

In shadowy ships, that freeze,
  We think of men who sail, the frozen-fated;
Tears, if you will, for these.
But, oh, the truest searcher of the seas
  In the blown breath of English daisies waited.

...A Pathway, here or there,
  He sought--the old, unlighted Pathway finding:
Out of the North's despair,
Out of the South's flower-burdened wastes of air,
  To that great Peaceful Sea forever winding.

  ...Oh, after her vague quest
  Among weird winds, in icy deserts, lonely,
Has she laid down to rest
Under a Palm, whose light leaves on her breast
  Drop balms of summer, sun and silence only?

Has some one whispered: "Why,
  O woman faithful, why this dark delaying
Outside the pleasant sky?--
How could you seek me in the snows, when I
  Here, in the Loveliest Land of all, was staying?"

1877

HER CROSS AND MINE

"This is my cross--here, Sister, see:
  The only one I have to bear."
A flash of gold fell over me,
  And precious lights were everywhere.

She was a lovely, restless thing,
  With time in blossom at her feet,
And on her hand the enchanted ring
  Whose promise always is so sweet.

I was a nun. My fearless eyes
  Had looked their last on youth. I guessed
At something quiet in the skies,
  And veiled my face against the rest.

My cross was dark and darkly stained,
  Even from the heart of one who died:
Invisible drops of blood had rained
  Thereon, when love was crucified.

That laughing girl could pity me,
  Because she fancied from my cross
The world had fallen. Such as she
  Still think to lose the world--is loss!

Yet, heavier is her cross than mine,
  For in the fatal jewels there
(Oh, will she ask for help divine?)
  I know she has the world to bear.

1877

COUNTING THE GRAVES

"How many graves are in this world?" "Oh, child,"
  His mother answered, "surely there are two."
Archly he shook his pretty head and smiled:
  "I mean in this whole world, you know I do!"

"Well, then, in this whole world: in East and West,
  In North and South, in dew and sand and snow,
In all sad places where the dead may rest:
  There are two graves--yes, there are two, I know."

"But graves have been here for a thousand years--
  Or, for ten thousand? Soldiers die, and kings;
And Christians die--sometimes." "My own poor ears
  Have never yet been troubled by these things.

..."More graves within the hollow ground, in sooth,
  Than there are stars in all the pleasant sky?--
Where did you ever learn such dreary truth,
  Oh, wiser and less selfish far than I?

"I did not know,--I who had light and breath:
  Something to touch, to look at, if no more.
Fair earth to live in, who believe in death,
  Till, dumb and blind, he lies at their own door?

..."I did not know--I may have heard or read--
  Of more; but should I search the wide grass through,
Lift every flower and every thorn," she said,
  "From every grave--oh, I should see but two!"

1875

104

WE TWO

God's will is--the bud of the rose for your hair,
 The ring for your hand and the pearl for your breast;
God's will is--the mirror that makes you look fair.
 No wonder you whisper: "God's will is the best."

But what if God's will were the famine, the flood?--
 And were God's will the coffin shut down in your face?--
And were God's will the worm in the fold of the bud,
 Instead of the picture, the light, and the lace?

Were God's will the arrow that flieth by night,
 Were God's will the pestilence walking by day,
The clod in the valley, the rock on the height--
 I fancy "God's will" would be harder to say.

God's will is--your own will. What honor have you
 For having your own will, awake or asleep?
Who praises the lily for keeping the dew,
 When the dew is so sweet for the lily to keep?

God's will unto me is not music or wine.
 With helpless reproaching, with desolate tears,
God's will I resist, for God's will is divine;
 And I--shall be dust to the end of my years.

God's will is--not mine. Yet one night I shall lie
 Very still at his feet, where the stars may not shine.
"Lo! I am well pleased," I shall hear from the sky;
 Because--it is God's will I do, and not mine.

1874

105

SAD WISDOM--FOUR YEARS OLD

"Well, but some time I will be dead;
   Then you will love me, too!"
Ah! mouth so wise for mouth so red,
   I wonder how you knew.
(Closer, closer, little brown head--
   Not long can I keep you!)

Here, take this one poor bud to hold
   Take this long kiss and last;
Love cannot loosen one fixed fold
   Of the shroud that holds you fast--
Never, never; oh, cold, so cold!
   All that was sweet is past.

Oh, tears, and tears, and foolish tears,
   Dropped on a grave somewhere!
Does not the child laugh in my ears
   What time I feign despair?
Whisper, whisper--I know he hears;
   Yet this is hard to bear.

O world, with your wet face above
   One veil of dust, thick-drawn!
O weird voice of the hapless dove,
   Broken for something gone!
Tell me, tell me, when will we love
   The thing the sun shines on?

1876

NO HELP

When will the flowers grow there? I cannot tell.
  Oh, many and many a rain will beat there first,
Stormy and dreary, such as never fell
  Save where the heart was breaking that had nursed
Something most dear a little while, and then
Murmured at giving God his own again.

The woods were full of violets, I know;
  And some wild sweet-briers grew so near the place:
Their time is not yet come. Dead leaves and snow
  Must cover first the darling little face
From these wet eyes, forever fixed upon
Your last still cradle, O most precious one!

Is he not with his Father? So I trust.
  Is he not His? Was he not also mine?
His mother's empty arms yearn toward the dust.
  Heaven lies too high, the soul is too divine.
I wake at night and miss him from my breast,
And--human words can never say the rest.

Safe? But out of the world, out of my sight!
  My way to him through utter darkness lies.
I am gone blind with weeping, and the light--
  If there be light--is shut inside the skies.
Think you, to give my bosom back his breath,
I would not kiss him from the peace called Death?

And do I want a little Angel? No,
  I want my Baby--with such piteous pain,
That were this bitter life thrice bitter, oh!
  I could not choose but take him back again.
God cannot help me, for God cannot break
His own dark Law--for my poor sorrow's sake.

1877

ASKING FOR TEARS

Oh, let me come to Thee in this wild way,
Fierce with a grief that will not sleep, to pray
Of all thy treasures, Father, only one,
After which I may say--Thy will be done.

Nay, fear not Thou to make my time too sweet.
I nurse a Sorrow,--kiss its hands and feet,
Call it all piteous, precious names, and try,
Awake at night, to hush its helpless cry.

The sand is at my moaning lip, the glare
Of the uplifted desert fills the air;
My eyes are blind and burning, and the years
Stretch on before me. Therefore, give me tears.

1877

CALLING THE DEAD

My little child, so sweet a voice might wake
So sweet a sleeper for so sweet a sake.
Calling your buried brother back to you,
You laugh and listen--till I listen too!

...Why does he listen? It may be to hear
Sounds too divine to reach my troubled ear.
Why does he laugh? It may be he can see
The face that only tears can hide from me.

Poor baby faith--so foolish or so wise:
The name I shape out of forlornest cries
He speaks as with a bird's or blossom's breath.
How fair the knowledge is that knows not Death!

...Ah, fools and blind--through all the piteous years
Searchers of stars and graves--how many seers,
Calling the dead, and seeking for a sign,
Have laughed and listened, like this child of mine?

1875

TRADITION OF CONQUEST

His Grace of Marlborough, legends say,
  Though battle-lightnings proved his worth,
Was scathed like others, in his day,
  By fiercer fires at his own hearth.

The patient chief, thus sadly tried--
  Madam, the Duchess, was so fair--
In Blenheim's honors felt less pride
  Than in the lady's lovely hair.

Once (shorn, she had coiled it there to wound
  Her lord when he should pass, 'tis said),
Shining across his path he found
  The glory of the woman's head.

No sudden word, nor sullen look,
  In all his after days, confessed
He missed the charm whose absence took
  A scar's pale shape within his breast.

I think she longed to have him blame,
  And soothe him with imperious tears--
As if her beauty were the same,
  He praised her through his courteous years.

But when the soldier's arm was dust,
  Among the dead man's treasures, where
He laid it as from moth and rust,
  They found his wayward wife's sweet hair.

1876

A DEAD MAN'S FRIENDS

Gathered from many lands,
  A company still and strange
  In the shadow of velvet and oak! --
  Not one to another spoke.
  With faces that did not change,
Weird with the night and dim,
They were looking their last at him.

If ever men were wise,
  If ever women were fair,
  If ever glory was dust
  In a world of moth and rust--
  Why these and this were there.
Guests of the great, ah me!
How cold is your courtesy!

Does the loveliest lady of all
  Drop Titian's light from her hair
  Down into his darkened eyes--
  His, who in his coffin lies?
  Does that crouching Venus care
That he must forget the charm
Of her broken, beautiful arm?

Yet these were the dead man's friends,
  Wooed in his passionate youth
  And won when his head was gray--
  Look at them close, I pray.
  Ah, these he has loved, in sooth;
Yet among them all, I fear,
Is nothing so sweet as--a tear!

1877

PEACE MAKING

After this feud of yours and mine,
    The sun will shine;
After we both forget, forget,
    The sun will set.

I pray you think how warm and sweet
    The heart can beat;
I pray you think how soon the rose
    From grave-dust grows.

1877

THE LITTLE BOY I DREAMED ABOUT

This is the only world I know--
  It is in this same world, no doubt.
Ah me, but I could love him so,
  If I could only find him out--
  The Little Boy I dreamed about!

This Little Boy, who never takes
  The prettiest orange he can see,
The reddest apple, all the cakes
  (When there are twice enough for three)--
  Where can the darling ever be?

He does not tease and storm and pout
  To climb the roof in rain or sun,
And pull the pigeon's feathers out
  To see how it will look with none,
  Or fight with hornets one to one!

He does not hide and cut his hair
  And wind the watches wrong, and cry
To throw the kitten down the stair
  And see how often it will die!
  (It's strange that you can wonder why!)

He never wakes too late to know
  A bird is singing near his bed;
He tells the tired moon: "You may go
  To sleep yourself." He never said,
  When told to do a thing, "Tell Fred!"

If I say, "Go," he will not stay
  To lose his hat, or break a toy;
Then hurry like the wind away,
  And whistle like the wind, for joy
  To please himself--this Little Boy.

Let any stranger come who can,
    He will not say--if it is true
"Old Lady" (or "Old Gentleman"),
    "I wish you would go home, I do--
    I think my mama wants you to!"

No--Fairyland is far and dim:
    He does not play in silver sand;
But if I could believe in him
    I could believe in Fairyland.
    Because---you do not understand.

Dead--dead? Somehow I do not know.
    The sweetest children die. We may
Miss some poor footprint from the snow,
    That was his very own today.
    "God's will"--is what the Christians say.

Like you, or you, or you can be
    When you are good, he looks, no doubt.
I'd give--the goldenest star I see
    In all the dark to find him out,
    The Little Boy I dreamed about!

1877

114

THE BABY'S HAND

What is it the Baby's hand can hold? --
  Only one little flower, do you say?
Why, all the blossoms that ever blew
In the sweet wide wind away from the dew,
And all the jewels and all the gold
  Of the kingdoms of the world today,
The Baby's hand can hold.

What is it the Baby's hand can hold?
  Why, all the honey of all the bees,
And all the valleys where summer stays,
And all the sands of the desert's ways,
And all the snows that were ever cold,
  And all the mountains and all the seas,
The Baby's hand can hold.

What is it the Baby's hand can hold--
  The Baby's hand so pretty and small?
Why, just what the shoulders of Atlas bear,
Bending him down in the picture there:
(Now all I can tell you is surely told)--
  "But that is the world?" Well, that is all
The Baby's hand can hold.

How is it the Baby's hand can hold
  The world? ---Yes, surely I ought to know;
For oh, were the Baby's hand withdrawn,
Down into the dust the world were gone,
Folded therein as you might fold
  The sad white bud of a rose--just so--
For the Baby's hand to hold.

1877

115

"MORE ABOUT THE FAIRIES"

In daisy-leaf dresses too pretty to touch,
    And little lace-wings made of dreams and of dew,
I think I have told you as much and as much
    Of these people of moonshine--as ever I knew!

"Then read about them in the Bible?" Look here,
    You smallest of saints (for your first name is Paul),
The truth is, if I can remember, I fear
    The Bible says nothing about them at all.

"Then when did God make them?" Why, when he made Eve
    They were hid in the lilies of Eden, I guess.
"But the Snake?"--Never mind; you and I will believe
    In the angels a little--the snake somewhat less!

You thought it was after the flood they were made
    (When the dove was so white and the sea was so dark),
Because there were none of them, you are afraid,
    With the other wild animals, saved in the ark!

"But if they are not in the Bible, why then
    They are not anywhere--for they cannot be true?"
They're in---next-to-the-Bible! The greatest of men
    Believed in them, surely, as much as you do.

You do not believe in them?--"It would be sin
    To believe in things out of the Bible?" Oh, dear!
Fair sir, are you not rather young to begin
    To be doubting the faith of--one Mr. Shakespeare?

... Still, sooner or later, Time touches the towers
    Where the Golden Hair used to glimmer so--
Then what is there left in this wide world of ours
    That we children care any longer to know?

... Go, then, and believe in the red on the rose,
   In the gold on the moon, in the butterfly's wings,
And believe, if you will, in--the wind as it blows
   The beauty away from all beautiful things!

1877

THE SAD STORY OF A LITTLE GIRL

Oh, never mind her eyes and hair
  (Though they were dark and it was gold!)
That she was sweet is all I care
  To tell you--till the rest is told.
  ---"But is the story old?"

Hush. She *was* sweet---Why do I cry?
  Because--her mother loved her so.
I told you that she did not die;
  But she is gone. "Where did she go?"
  Ah me,--I do not know.

"How old was she when she was sweet?"
  Why, one year old, or two, or three.
Here is her shoe--what little feet!
  And yet they walked away, you see.
  (I must not say, from me.)

"Did Gypsies take her?" Surely, no.
  But--something took her; she is lost:
No track of hers in dew or snow,
  No heaps of wild buds backward tossed,
  To show what paths she crossed.

"Did Fairies take her?" It may be.
  For Fairies sometimes, I have read,
Will climb the moonshine, secretly,
  To steal a baby from its bed,
  And leave an imp instead.

This Changeling, German tales declare,
  Makes trouble in the house full soon:
Cries at the tangles in its hair,
  Beats the piano out of tune,
  And--wants to sleep till noon.

And, while it keeps the lost one's face,
  It grows less lovely, year by year--
Yes, in the pretty baby's place
    There was a Changeling left, I fear.
    ...My little maid, do you hear?

1877

REPROOF TO A ROSE

Sad rose, foolish rose,
        Fading on the floor,
Will he love you while he knows
        There are many more
        At the very door?

Sad rose, foolish rose,
        One among the rest:
Each is lovely--each that blows;
        It must be confest
        None is loveliest.

Sad rose, foolish rose,
        Had you known to wait,
And with dead leaves or with snows
        Come alone and late--
        Sweet had been your fate!

Sad rose, foolish rose,
        If no other grew
In the wide world, I suppose
        My own lover, too,
        Would love--only you!

1879

A PIQUE AT PARTING

Why, sir, as to that--I did not know it was time for
                                    the moon to rise,
  (So, the longest day of them all can end, if we will have
                                    patience with it.)
One woman can hardly care, I think, to remember another
                                    one's eyes,
      And--the bats are beginning to flit.
      ... We hate one another? It may be true.
      What else do you teach us to do?
      Yes, verily, to love you.

My lords--and gentlemen--are you sure that after we love
                                    quite all
  There is in your noble selves to be loved, no time on
                                    our hands will remain?
Why, an hour a day were enough for this. We may watch the
                                    wild leaves fall
      On the graves you forget.... It is plain
      That you were not pleased when she said--Just so;
      Still, what do we want, after all, you know,
      But room for a rose to grow?

You leave us the baby to kiss, perhaps; the bird in the cage
                                    to sing;
  The flower on the window, the fire on the hearth (and the
                                    fires in the heart) to tend.
When the wandering hand that would reach somewhere has become
                                    the Slave of the Ring,
      You give us--an image to mend;
      Then shut with a careless smile, the door--
      (There's dew or frost on the path before)
      We are safe inside. What more?

If the baby should moan, or the bird sit hushed, or the flower
                    fade out--what then?
    Ah? the old, old feud of mistress and maid would be left
                    though the sun went out?
You can number the stars and call them by names, and, as men,
                    you can wring from men
            The world--for they own it, no doubt.
            We, not being eagles, are doves? Why, yes,
            We must hide in the leaves, I guess,
            And coo down our loneliness.

God meant us for saints? Yes--in Heaven. Well, I, for one,
                    am content
    To trust Him through darkness and space to the end--if an end
                    there shall be;
But, as to His meanings, I fancy I never knew quite what
                    He meant.
            And--why, what were you saying to me
            Of the saints--or that saint? It is late;
            The lilies look weird by the gate.
            ...Ah, sir, as to that--we will wait.

                            1880

THE DESCENT OF THE ANGEL

"This is the house. Come, take the keys.
    Romance and Travel here must end."
 Out of the clouds, not quite at ease,
    I saw the pretty bride descend;
 With satin sandals, fit alone
 To glide in air, she touched the stone.

 A thing to fade through wedding lace,
    From silk and scents, with priest and ring,
 Floated across that earthly place
    Where life must be an earthly thing.
 An earthly voice was in her ears,
 Her eyes awoke to earthly tears.

1879

HER WORD OF REPROACH

We must not quarrel, whatever we do;
  For if I was (but I was not!) wrong,
Here are the tears for it, here are the tears:--
  What else has a woman to offer you?
Love might not last for a thousand years,
  You know, though the stars should rise so long.

Oh you, you talk in a man's great way!--
  So, love would last though the stars should fall?
Why, yes. If it last to the grave, indeed,
  After the grave last on it may.
But--in the grave? Will its dust take heed
  Of anything sweet--or the sweetest of all?

Ah, death is nothing! It may be so.
  Yet, granting at least that death is death
(Pray, look at the rose, and hear the bird),
  Whatever it is--we must die to know!
Sometime we may long to say one word
  Together--and find we have no breath.

Ah me, how divine you are growing again!--
  How coldly sure that the Heavens are sure,
Whither too lightly you always fly
  To hide from the passion of human pain.
Come, grieve that the Earth is not secure,
  For this one night--and forget the sky!

1880

CAPRICE AT HOME

No, I will not say good-by--
  Not good-by, nor anything.
He is gone... I wonder why
  Lilacs are not sweet this spring.
  How that tiresome bird will sing!

I might follow him and say
  Just that he forgot to kiss
Baby, when he went away.
  Everything I want I miss.
  Oh, a precious world is this!

...What if night came and not he?
  Something might mislead his feet.
Does the moon rise late? Ah me!
  There are things that he might meet.
  Now the rain begins to beat:

So it will be dark. The bell?--
  Some one some one loves is dead.
Were it he--! I cannot tell
  Half the fretful words I said,
  Half the fretful tears I shed.

Dead? And but to think of death!--
  Men might bring him through the gate:
Lips that have not any breath,
  Eyes that stare-- And I must wait!
  Is it time, or is it late?

I was wrong, and wrong, and wrong;
  I will tell him, oh, be sure!
If the heavens are builded strong,
  Love shall therein be secure;
  Love like mine shall there endure.

...Listen, listen--that is he!
I'll not speak to him, I say.
If he choose to say to me,
"I was all to blame today;
Sweet, forgive me," why--I may!

1877

A GHOST AT THE OPERA

It was, I think, the Lover of the play:
  He, from stage-incantations, turned his head,
And one remember'd motion shook away
  The whole mock fairyland and raised the dead.

I, in an instant, saw the scenery change.
  Old trees before me by enchantment grew.
Late roses shivered, beautiful and strange.
  One red geranium scented all the dew.

A sudden comet flung its awful veil
  Around the frightened stars. A sudden light
Stood, moon-shaped, in the East. A sudden wail
  From troubled music smote the spectral night.

Then blue sweet shadows fell from flower-like eyes,
  And purplish darkness droop'd on careless hair,
And lips most lovely--ah, what empty sighs,
  Breathed to the air, for something less than air!

Oh, beauty such as no man ever wore
  In this wan world outside of Eden's shine,
Save he who vanished from the sun before
  Youth learn'd that youth itself was not divine!

I might have touch'd that fair and real ghost,
  He laugh'd so lightly, look'd so bright and brave--
So all unlike that thin and wavering host
  Who walk unquiet from the quiet grave.

Myself another ghost as vain and young,
  And nearer Heaven than now by years and years,
My heart, like some quick bird of morning, sung
  On fluttering wings above all dust and tears.

But some great lightning made a long red glare:
  Black-plumed and brigand-like I saw him stand--
What ghastly sights, what noises in the air!
  How sharp the sword seemed in his lifted hand!

He looked at me across the fading field.
  The South was in his blood, his soul, his face.
Imperious despair, too lost to yield,
  Gave a quick glory to a desperate grace.

I saw him fall. I saw the deadly stain
  Upon his breast--he cared not what was won.
The ghost was in the land of ghosts again.
  The curtain fell, the phantom play was done.

1873

A LESSON IN A PICTURE

So it is whispered, here and there,
   That you are rather pretty? Well?
(Here's matter for a bird of the air
   To drop down from the dusk and tell.)
Let's have no lights, my child. Somehow,
The shadow suits your blushes now.

The blonde young man who called today
   (He only rang to leave a book?--
Yes, and a flower or two, I say!)
   Was handsome, look you. Will you look?
You did not know his eyes were fine?--
You did not? Can you look in mine?

What is it in this picture here,
   That you should suddenly watch it so?
A maiden leaning, half in fear,
   From her far casement; and, below,
In cap and plumes (or cap and bells?)
Some fairy tale her lover tells.

Suppose this lonesome night could be
   Some night a thousand springs ago,
Dim round that tower; and you were she,
   And your shy friend her lover (Oh!)
And I--her mother! And suppose
I knew just why she wore that rose.

Do you think I'd kiss my girl, and say:
   "Make haste to bid the wedding guest,
And make the wedding garment gay.
   You could not find in East or West
So brave a bridegroom; I rejoice
That you have made so sweet a choice"?

Or say, "To look forever fair,
  Just keep this turret moonlight wound
About your face; stay in mid-air;--
  Rope-ladders lead one to the ground,
Where all things take the touch of tears,
And nothing lasts a thousand years"?

1879

AFTER THE QUARREL

Hush, my pretty one. Not yet.
  Wait a little, only wait.
Other blue flowers are as wet
  As your eyes, outside the gate
He has shut forever. --But
Is the gate forever shut?

Just a young man in the rain
  Saying (the last time?) "good-night!"
Should he never come again
  Would the world be ended quite?
Where would all these rose-buds go?--
All these robins? Do you know?

But--he will not come? Why, then,
  Is no other within call?
There are men, and men, and men--
  And these men are brothers all!
Each sweet fault of his you'll find
Just as sweet in all his kind.

None with eyes like his? Oh--oh!
  In diviner ones did I
Look, perhaps, an hour ago,
  Whose? Indeed (you must not cry)
Those I thought of--are not free
To laugh down your tears, you see.

Voice like his was never heard?
  No--but better ones, I vow;
Did you ever hear a bird?--
  Listen, one is singing now!
And his gloves? His gloves? Ah, well,
There are gloves like his to sell.

At the play tonight you'll see,
  In mock-velvet cloaks, mock earls
With mock-jewelled swords, that he
  Were a clown by! Now, those curls
Are the barber's pride, I say;
Do not cry for them, I pray.

If no one should love you? Why,
  You can love some other still:
Philip Sidney, Shakespeare, ay,
  Good King Arthur, if you will;
Raphael--*he* was handsome too.
Love them one and all. I do.

1878

"TO BE DEAD"

If I should have void darkness in my eyes
  While there were violets in the sun to see;
If I should fail to hear my child's sweet cries,
  Or any bird's voice in our threshold tree;

If I should cease to answer love or wit:
  Blind, deaf, or dumb, how bitter each must be!
Blind, deaf, or dumb--I will not think of it!
  ... Yet the night comes when I shall be all three.

1877

THE BABY'S BROTHER

The Baby is brought for the lady to see;
"Was ever a lily-bud nicer than he?"
But the door opens fiercely on cooing and kiss,
And--what merry outlaw from the greenwood is this?

His brother?--who laughs at himself in my face:
This picturesque vagabond, graceless with grace,
Whose head, like a king's come to grief, is discrowned--
Ah, the kitten was wicked, and so she is drowned?

All flushed with the butterfly chase, how he stands,
With a nestful of birds in his pitiless hands,
Which he mildly assures me were torn from the tree,
Or they'd trouble their mother as Baby does me!

"Well, if Baby is sweet, you must love him right fast,
Because--don't you know? Why, because he'll not last!
For I was a baby, too, some of these days,
And just look at me now!" he unsparingly says.

1880

ONE YEAR OLD

So, now he has seen the sun and the moon,
　The flower and the falling leaf on the tree
(Ah, the world is a picture that's looked at soon),
　Is there anything more to see?

He has learned (let me kiss from his eyes that tear),
　As the children tell me, to creep and to fall;--
Then life is a lesson that's taught in a year,
　For the baby knows it all.

1880

CHILD'S-FAITH

These beautiful tales, I trust, are true.
  But here is a grave in the moss,
And there is the sky. And the buds are blue,
  And a butterfly blows across.

Yes, here is the grave and there is the sky;--
  To the one or the other we go.
And between them wavers the butterfly,
  Like a soul that does not know,

Somewhere? Nowhere? Too-golden head,
  And lips that I miss and miss,
You would tell me the secret of the dead--
  Could I find you with a kiss!

...Come here, I say, little child of mine,
  Come with your bloom and breath.
(If he should believe in the life divine,
  I will not believe in death!)

"Where is your brother?"--I question low,
  And wait for his wise reply.
Does he say, "Down there in the grave?" Ah, no--
  He says, with a laugh, "In the sky!"

1877

THE SIGHT OF TROUBLE

So, then, my boy, you want to know
  Just what is trouble? Some great day, no doubt,
When all this world is full of rain or snow,
Or lonesomer because the birds sing so;
Or some strange night, when this same moon drops low
  On many graves--or one--you will find out.

You do not want to wait, I fear--
  You want to see it now, or pretty soon?
The woman dressed in black so who was here
Said she saw trouble always? It is queer
That she sees things you cannot see, my dear.
  ---Did I say there was trouble in the moon?

No, but I think it may be there,
  For people see it when they lie awake.
And in the sun as well, and in the air,
And in the tangles of some yellow hair,
And in the wind that blows it everywhere--
  Except to Heaven (if I do not mistake).

Once when her boy was dead, ah, me!
  It would not let her sleep?---Is it a ghost?
Why, if it were a ghost, then it would be
Something, or nothing, that we cannot see!
And yet it is a ghost, sometimes, and we
  Just think we see it, in the dark, at most.

Do women, then, wear glasses so
  They can see trouble? Hardly, I'm afraid;
Perhaps they see it plainer with them, though.
Oh, as to men! Indeed, I do not know.
They miss the train because their watch is slow,
  And drink such coffee as was never made;

They have to wait till some one brings
  Their hat and gloves and overcoat and all,
After that terrible last church-bell rings,
While she is only doing fifty things
Between the tying of her bonnet-strings,
  The baby's cries, and putting on her shawl.

So these poor men see trouble too,
  In their own way, a little, I suppose.
Still, what is trouble? Just see here, if you
Tore off that first white rose before I knew
How sweet it was, and cut this lace all through,
  Too well I know how well your mother knows.

1880

A HINT FROM HOMER

(Their Heroic Lesson)

I let the sun stand still, this lonesome day,
  And hardly heard the very baby coo,
(Meanwhile the world went on--the other way!)
  That I might watch the siege of Troy with you.

The great Achilles (whom we knew) was there--
  His shining shield was what we knew him by;
And Hector with his plume of horse's hair
  Frightened his child and laughed to hear it cry.

Poor Hector! Never sorrow for the dead,
  In these three thousand rather piteous years,
Stole into sweeter words than Helen said
  Beside him, through the dropping of her tears.

We grieved with Priam for his gracious son.
  Much-wandering Ulysses with his craft
Cheated us through strange seas--and every one
  Came straight to grief with him upon his raft.

Not one among you but could draw his bow,
  After its rest in Ithaca, and bring
A suitor down! --In the dark backward, oh,
  How sad the swallow-twitter of its string!

Now, that it's time to shut the shadowy book,
  (Ah me, they clash together, left and right,
And Greek meets Greek--or Trojan! Only look!)--
  What have you learned from it? You say: "To fight!"

1878

IN CLONMEL PARISH CHURCHYARD

(At the Grave of Charles Wolfe)

Where the graves were many, we looked for one.
 Oh, the Irish rose was red,
And the dark stones saddened the setting sun
 With the names of the early dead.
Then a child who, somehow, had heard of him
 In the land we love so well,
Kept lifting the grass till the dew was dim
 In the churchyard of Clonmel.

But the sexton came. "Can you tell us where
 Charles Wolfe is buried?" "I can--
See, that is his grave in the corner there.
 (Ay, he was a clever man,
If God had spared him!) It's many that come
 To be asking for him," said he.
But the boy kept whispering, "Not a drum
 Was heard," --in the dusk to me.

(Then the gray man tore a vine from the wall
 Of the roofless church where he lay,
And the leaves that the withering year let fall
 He swept, with the ivy away;
And, as we read on the rock the words
 That, writ in the moss, we found,
Right over his bosom a shower of birds
 In music fell to the ground).

... Young poet, I wonder did you care,
 Did it move you in your rest
To hear that child in his golden hair,
 From the mighty woods of the West,
Repeating your verse of his own sweet will,
 To the sound of the twilight bell,
Years after your beating heart was still
 In the churchyard of Clonmel?   1883

A CALL ON SIR WALTER RALEIGH

(At Youghal, County Cork)

"Ay, not at home, then didst thou say?
  --And, prithee, hath he gone to court?"
"Nay; he hath sailed but yesterday,
  With Edmund Spenser, from this port.

"This Spenser, folk do say, hath writ
  Twelve cantos, called 'The Faerie Queene'
To seek for one to publish it,
  They go--on a long voyage, I ween."

Ah me! I came so far to see
  This ruffed and plumed cavalier--
He whom romance and history,
  Alike, to all the world make dear.

And I had some strange things to tell
  Of our New World, where he hath been;
And now they say--I marked them well--
  They say the Master is not in!

The knaves speak not the truth; I see
  Sir Walter at the window there.
--That is the hat, the sword, which he
  In pictures hath been pleased to wear.

There hangs the very cloak whereon
  Elizabeth set foot. (But oh,
Young diplomat, as things have gone,
  Pity it is she soiled it so!)

And there--but look! he's lost in smoke:
  (That weirdly charmed Virginia weed!)
Make haste, bring anything; his cloak--
  They save him with a shower, indeed!

...Ay, lost in smoke. I linger where
  He walked his garden. Day is dim,
And death-sweet scents rise to the air
  From flowers that gave their breath to him.

There, with its thousand years of tombs,
  The dark church glimmers where he prayed;
Here, with that high head shorn of plumes,
  The tree he planted gave him shade.

That high head shorn of plumes? Even so
  It stained the Tower, when gray with grief.
O tree he planted, as I go,
  For him I tenderly take a leaf.

I have been dreaming here, they say,
  Of one dead knight forgot at court.
--And yet he sailed but yesterday,
  With Edmund Spenser, from this port.

1883

A CHILD'S CRY

(At Kilcolman Castle, March 1883)

I do not meet him in his place
   (Nor miss him) I, who came to meet
At his own hearth, and face to face,
   A poet, world-beloved, whose feet
Here, walking toward Westminster's gloom,
Left daisies in their prints to bloom.

I do not miss him, though I look
   From windows where he watched, and try--
Ah me!--to think about his book.
   ...There lie his hills, his streams, the high
Far singer, whose divine old song
Was--well, perhaps almost too long!

Hush! (Do I hear his grave sweet words
   To Walter Raleigh on the stair?)
--"You hear the little Irish birds;
   They're singing all at once out there,"
The children said; "we made them fly
Out of the ivy." ...No, not I.

It is---I tell you it might break
   One's heart to hear it! Listen. Oh,
It is a child's cry, scared awake
   By soldiers trampling to and fro:
The baby by its father's flight
Left--to the fire--at dead of night!

At dead of night it was. And still
   (Oh, burning cradle--foolish tears!)
At dead of night---but doubt who will,
   I hear it, through three hundred years.
And all the music Spenser writ
Is as a whisper now to it!

                              1885

143

COMFORT THROUGH A WINDOW

(Child Within To Tramp Without)

It's not so nice here as it looks,
  With china that keeps breaking so,
And five of Mr. Tennyson's books
  Too fine to look in--is it, though?

If you just had to sit here (Well!)
  In satin chairs too blue to touch,
And look at flowers too sweet to smell,
  In vases--would you like it much?

If you see any flowers, they grow,
  And you can find them in the sun.
These are the ones we buy, you know,
  In winter-time--when there are none!

Then you can sit on rocks, you see,
  And walk about in water, too--
Because you have no shoes! Dear me!
  How many things they let you do!

Then you can sleep out in the shade
  All day, I guess, and all night too,
Because--you know, you're not afraid
  Of other fellows just like you!

You have no house like this, you know,
  (Where mamma's cross, and ladies call)--
You have the world to live in, though,
  And that's the prettiest place of all!

1885

144

THE THOUGHT OF ASTYANAX BESIDE IULUS

(After reading Virgil's story of Andromache in Exile)

Yes, all the doves begin to moan--
But it is not the doves alone.
Some trouble, that you never heard
In any tree from breath of bird,
That reaches back to Eden lies
Between your wind-flower and my eyes.

I fear it was not well, indeed,
Upon so sad a day to read
So sad a story. But the day
Is full of blossoms, do you say--
And how the sun does shine? I know.
These things do make it sadder, though.

You'd cry, if you were not a boy,
About this mournful tale of Troy?
Then do not laugh at me, if I--
Who am too old, you know, to cry--
Just hide my face a while from you,
Down here among these drops of dew.

...Must I for sorrow look so far?
This baby headed like a star,
Afraid of Hector's horse-hair plume
(His one sweet child, whose bitter doom
So piteous seems--oh, tears and tears!--)
Has he been dust three thousand years?

Yet when I see his mother fold
The pretty cloak she stitched with gold,
Around another boy, and say:
"He would be just your age today,
With just your hands, your eyes, your hair"--
Her grief is more than I can bear.

                                    1885

A NEIGHBOURHOOD INCIDENT

"Did you know, Mamma, that the man was dead
  In that pretty place, there under the hill?"
"So, with only the clouds to cover his head,
  He died down there in that old stone mill;
He died, in the wind and sleet, and--mark
This truth, fair sirs--in the dark.

"(Yes, a pretty place!) In the summer-time,
  When the birds sing out of the leaves for joy,
And the blue wild morning-glories climb
  On the broken walls, it is pretty, my boy:
But not when the world around is snow
And the river is ice below.

"Men looked sometimes from the morning cars
  Toward the place where he lay in the winter sun,
And said, through the smoke of their dear cigars,
  That something really ought to be done.
Then talked of the President, or the play,
Or the war--that was farthest away."

"Do you know when his father wanted some bread,
  One time, by the well there? Wasn't he old!
I mean that day when the blossoms were red
  On the cliffs, and it wasn't so very cold."
"And I gave him the little I well could spare
When I looked at his face and hair.

"Then we met him once--it was almost night--
  Out looking for berries among the briers,
So withered and weird, such a piteous sight,
  And gathering wood for their gypsy fires.
'No, the young man is no better. No, no,'
He would keep on saying, so low."

146

"But the women there would not work, they say."
  "Why, that is the story; but, if it be true,
There are other women, I think, today
  Who will not work, yet, their whole lives through,
All lovely things from the seas and lands
Drop into their idle hands.

"But these would not work, so their brother--and ours--
  Deserved to die in that desolate place?
Shall we send regrets and the usual flowers?
  Shall we stop and see the upbraiding face,
As it lies in the roofless room forlorn,
For the sake of a dead man's scorn?

"He did his best, as none will deny,
  At serving the Earth to pay for his breath;
So she gave him early (and why not, why?)
  The one thing merciful men call Death.
Ah! gift that must be gracious indeed,
Since it leaves us nothing to need!

"...As for us, sweet friends, let us dress and sleep,
  Let us praise our pictures and drink our wine.
Meanwhile, let us drive His starving sheep
  To our good Lord Christ, on the heights divine;
For the flowerless valleys are dim and drear,
And the winds right bitter, down here."

North Bend, Ohio   1885

147

HIS MOTHER'S WAY

"My Mamma just knows how to cry
  About an old glove or a ring,
Or even a stranger going by
  The gate, or--almost anything!

"She cried till both her eyes were red
  About <u>him</u>, too. (I saw her, though!)
And he was just a _____, Papa said.
  (We have to call them that, you know.)

"She cried about the shabbiest shawl,
  Because it cost too much to buy;
But Papa cannot cry at all,
  For he's a man. And that is why!

"Why, if his coat was not right new,
  And if the yellow bird would die
That sings, and my white kitten too,
  Or even himself, <u>he</u> would not cry.

"He said that he would sleep tonight
  With both the pistols at his head,
Because that ragged fellow might
  Come back. That's what my Papa said!

"But Mamma goes and hides her face
  There in the curtains, and peeps out
At him, and almost spoils the lace--
  And he is what she cries about!

"She says he looks so cold, so cold,
  And has no pleasant place to stay!
Why can't he work? He is not old;
  His eyes are blue--they've not turned grey."

So the boy babbled.... Well, sweet sirs,
  Flushed with your office-fires you write
Your laugh down at such grief as hers;
  But are these women foolish quite?

---I know. But, look you, there may be
  Stains sad as wayside dust, I say,
Upon your own white hands (ah, me!)
  No woman's tears can wash away.

One sees her baby's dimple hold
  More love than you can measure.... Then
Nights darken down on heads of gold,
  Till wind and frost try wandering men!

But there are prisons made for such,
  Where the strong roof shuts out the snow;
And bread (that you would scorn to touch)
  Is served them there? I know, I know.

Ah! while you have your books, your ease,
  Your lamp-light leisure, jests, and wine,
Fierce outside whispers, if you please,
  Moan, each: "These things are also mine!"

1880

IN STREET AND GARDEN

I.

A Child's Conclusion

"Mamma," he said, "you ought to know
The place. Its name is wicked, though.
Not China. No. But if you fell
Through China you would be there! Well.

"Fred said somebody very bad,
Named Satan, stayed down there, and had
Oh, such a fire to burn things! You
Just never mind. It can't be true.

"Because I've digged and digged to see
Where all that fire could ever be,
And looked and looked down through the dark,
And never saw a single spark.

"But Heaven is sure; because if I
Look up, I always see the sky--
Sometimes the gold-gates shine clear through--
And when you see a thing, it's true!"

1885

THE CHRISTENING

In vain we broider cap and cloak, and fold
  The long robe, white and rare;
In vain we serve on dishes of red gold,
  Perhaps, the rich man's fare;
In vain we bid the fabled folk who bring
  All gifts the world holds sweet:
This one, forsooth, shall give the child to sing;
  To move like music this shall charm its feet;
  This help the cheek to blush, the heart to beat.

Unto the christening there shall surely come
  The Uninvited Guest,
The evil mother, weird and wise, with some
  Sad purpose in her breast.
Yes, and though every spinning-wheel be stilled
  In all the country round,
Behold, the prophecy must be fulfilled;
  The turret with the spindle will be found,
  And the white hand will reach and take the wound.

1884

A PORTRAIT AT YOUGHAL

There at the inn, he looked at me.
  A flash of fire died on the wall.
Without, the broken-hearted sea
  Beat in the moon at Youghal.

Still as a god's were those deep eyes,
  And empty as a god's of tears,
That showed nor pity nor surprise
  After three hundred years.

I felt that one pale flower's sharp scent
  There at the window like a knife,
What time the dead man seemed content
  To watch the passion of life.

Another flash of fire. --And so
  They've given us a haunted room:
The knight there in the dusk bowed low--
  Or the wind waved his plume!

...But what is this? --The maid with tea.
  (It may be she has heard the name
This dark immortal wore while he
  Walked in the world's brief fame.)

"Who is it--that old portrait--there?"
  She held the lamp close to the wall,
And told us, with a little stare,
  "He was--the Mayor of Youghal."

1883

TWO INNOCENTS ABROAD

(On Coronation Day, June 1884)

Then all at once the loyal cannon spoke
  Across the hazy, old-world terraced town,
In bloom with British flags--where dust and smoke
          Have settled down.

Toward Camden and Spike Island looking out,
  Two children in the foreign sun lay curled:
"Oh listen, will you? What's the noise about?
          It shakes the world."

"The world don't mind it very much, I'd say--
  It doesn't sound much louder than a bee!
Why, I can hardly hear it. Any way,
          It don't shake me!"

"I'll tell you now, just what it all must mean,"
  Said little six-years-old: "I think it's--War."
"No, it's--the English, for their gracious Queen
          And Governor!

"This is the very day she first put on
  The crown. And, if the Irish like or not,
Somebody's got to wear it till it's gone,
          And that is what!"

"Well, what day did the President, you know,
  Put on his crown?" "To hear you talk like that!
The President's a gentleman--and so
          He wears a hat.

"You know the crown. We saw it in the Tower."
  "But was it gold, or only shining brass--"
"(We had to look at it for half-an-hour!)--"
          "And painted glass?"

"The glass was only diamonds. But the gold
   Is sure enough. And it won't do to touch."
"It's shut up in a cage." "It is so old
                  It can't stand much!"

"I wish the President wore one." "He dare
   Not." "But, you know, it's prettier than a hat."
"You don't think any man alive would wear
                  A thing like that!

"The Queen's a lady. Don't you know that yet?"
   "I'd think that even the English wouldn't care
To have a lady for the Queen! I'd get
                  A man--somewhere!"

"The men are all in Egypt! (I suppose
   The English think they know what they're about.)
And General Gordon's--where nobody knows,
                  And can't get out!"

                              1886

                              154

THE WITCH IN THE GLASS

"My mother says I must not pass
    Too near that glass;
  She is afraid that I will see
  A little witch that looks like me,
  With a red, red mouth to whisper low
  The very thing I should not know!"

"Alack for all your mother's care!
    A bird of the air,
  A wistful wind, or (I suppose
  Sent by some hapless boy) a rose,
  With breath too sweet, will whisper low
  The very thing you should not know!"

1889

THE SERMON OF A STATUE

(In Westminster Abbey)

Suddenly, in the melancholy place
  With sculptured king and priest and knight assembled,
The music called us. Then, with kindly grace,
  On a gold head was laid a hand that trembled:
"You little stranger, come," the verger cried,
"And hear the sermon." "No," the child replied--

A moment standing on his New-World will,
  There in the Corner of the Poets, holding
His cap with pretty reverence, as still
  As any of that company, he said, folding
His arms: "But let that canon wait." And then:
"I want to stay here with these marble men--

"If they could preach, I'd listen!" Ah, they can,
  Another thought. It pleased the boy to linger
In the pale presence of the peerless man
  Who pointed to his text with moveless finger.
Laughing with blue-eyed wonder, he said: "Look,
This one (but do you know him?) has a book!"

...I know him. Ay, and all the world knows him--
  Among the many poets the one only!
On that high head the stained gloom was dim;
  In those fixed eyes the look of gods was lonely.
Kings at his feet, to whom his hand gave fame,
Lay, dust and ashes, shining through his name.

I heard him. With the still voice of the dead
  From that stone page, right careless of derision,
Sad jesters of a faithless age! he read
  How the great globe would vanish like a vision,
With all that it inhabit. ...And hath he
Then writ but one word, and that--Vanity?

1886

156

AFTER HER FIRST PARTY

"It was just lovely, and, mamma, my dress
  Was much the prettiest there, the boys all said:
They said too that I looked--my best. I guess
  These ribbons suited me. You see, that red,
You did not fancy, lighted up so well.
Somebody told me I was quite a belle.

"I wish you didn't want me to wear white,
  With just a flower or two. Rose wears such things.
They're so old-fashioned. She was such a fright!
  I wish that I had fifty diamond rings--
I'd wear them all at once! I'd almost paint,
Before I'd look like Rose. She's such a saint."

"I thought you were the best of friends." "We are--
  Only we hate each other! That is what
The best of friends do--in our school. How far
  Away you look! Forgive me. I forgot.
I've made you sad. *I'll* love the whole world too,
I guess, mamma--when I'm as old as you!

"Why don't you listen, mamma? You must be
  Thinking of Adam. Here's a bud he gave
You once in Eden--shut up here, you see,
  In this old book!" "That grew upon a grave."
"Oh, I'll not touch it, then. I wish that pearls
Would grow on trees--but not for other girls.

"Now, mamma, please to hear me to the end.
  The handsomest of all the boys last night
Looked like that picture of--your brother's friend.
  He hardly spoke to Rose. (Oh, I'm not quite
An angel yet. I shall be, I suppose,
Sometime.) I'm glad he hardly spoke to Rose.

"I wonder, mamma, did you ever go
    To a first party. And what did you wear?
---How odd you must have looked! But tell me, though,
    About your dress. How many girls were there?"
"Fifty, perhaps." "There were some boys, I'd guess?"
"Yes, there was one"-- "And he was handsome?" "Yes."

"Where is he now, do you think?" "I do not know.
    (In some sweet foreign country, it may be,
  Among the palms.") "He might have written, though,
    In all these years." "He cannot write." "I see.
  What a strange party! Fifty girls--oh dear!
  And one boy--and he couldn't write? How queer!"

                                        1889

A TRIUMPH OF TRAVEL

(At Edinburgh)

There rose the tragic palace towers
  Against the moon. (The tale was true!)
The Prince's Gardens faint with flowers
  And still with statue-spectres grew.

There, on its rock, the Castle lay,
  An awful shadow-shape forlorn,
Among the night-lamps, and, by day--
  The place where James the First was born.

There, for the Covenanters' sake,
  One haunts the grasses of Grey Friars;
There grim John Knox had loved to shake
  His right hand full of ghostly fires.

There, changed to marble, Walter Scott
  Received the world. And Burns of Ayr,
With all his loves and debts forgot,
  A bronze immortal met you there.

No whit the seven years' stranger cared;
  As under gables high and still
Through immemorial dust he fared,
  He spoke his heart out with a will:

"I'm tired of Holyrood, that's what!
  And all the other things," he said;
"There's nothing in it! She is not--
  I mean Queen Mary. She is dead.

"I'm glad I did just one thing there."
  (In vain they showed him "Rizzio's bluid.")
"I put my hand on every chair
  That said 'Don't Touch' at Holyrood!"

                                          1889

159

THE STORY OF A STORM

(Told by a Little Boy Who Had Heard "Stories from Homer")

"Things floated away and the day turned dark
  And papa he wasn't at home, you know;
And we didn't have any dove or ark,
  Nor mountain where we could go,
Like they used to have, one other year--
That time when the other flood was here.

"Then, the wind kept blowing the oak-tree down,
  (The Lord didn't know about the nest!)
And I thought this world was going to drown.
  --Did Louis tell you the rest?
Well, if he didn't--well then--well,
I think--Somebody will have to tell.

"Now, this was the way: One other night
  (I wish that Louis had told you then)
When the moon was red--why, we had a fight
  About one of Homer's men.
(That is the reason we didn't speak.)
He said that Hector wasn't a Greek!

"But I thought it wouldn't do to die
  And not say even one single word
To Louis before I went to the sky--
  So I told him about the bird,
And the other birds out there in the nest
That their mother hadn't even dressed!

"If it hadn't been for the rain, you see,
  We never could have been friends again.
And, who would I have to play with me--
  If it hadn't been for the rain?
And Louis said he was glad to speak,
For he <u>thought</u> that Hector wasn't a Greek!"

1889

160

THE COMING OUT OF HER DOLL

(Young Girl-Graduate To Her Mother)

"Now I begin to think it's time that Rose
   Should wear a train. She's a young lady now.
You really cannot guess how much she knows.
   (She's read some charming novels, anyhow.)

"How sweet she'd look in a Commencement dress,
   White satin and illusion, and some pearls.
Her gloves must have six buttons, and--I guess
   She'd get more flowers than all the other girls.

"I fancy she should have some company.
   (Papa, he always comes home late and tired.)
And if she only had--some one, you see,
   To take her out, she would be much admired.

"Oh, you forget. You brought her home to me
   Once on my birthday, years and years ago.
She could not be a baby yet, you see--
   Why, then I was a child myself, you know!"

1889

REQUIESCAT

Lie still. You need not love nor gold
  Nor name, to make the sum complete.
The world no living hand may hold
  Falls at a dead man's feet.

Lie still. You climbed for flowers, and found
  They grow not well in highest air.
Lie still: the rock, the thorn, the wound
  Were yours--you had your share.

Lie still. This is the end, they say.
  Lie still. The peasant and the king,
A little weary, walk this way;
  The bride leaves here her ring.

Your virtues? Though the priest speak true,
  You need not blush--your face is hid.
The roses life denied to you
  Are on your coffin lid.

1877

AT THE GRAVE OF A SUICIDE

You sat in judgment on him, you whose feet
  Were set in pleasant places, you who found
The Bitter Cup he dared to break still sweet,
  And shut him from your consecrated ground.

Yet, if you think the dead man sleeps a whit
  Less soundly in his grave, come look, I pray.
A violet has consecrated it.
  Henceforth you need not fear to walk this way.

1886

THE NIGHT-MOTH'S COMMENT

(Alighted upon a Yellow Autograph Letter of Chesterfield)

Here is a gracious letter that one writ
  Who thought this rugged world of lands and seas,
Among whose suns and rains we shadows flit--
  In sorrow and in mystery, if you please--
  A place to be polite and take one's ease.

My lord, above your old, dead courtesy,
  Out of the light of stars, in lovelier light,
All summer-green and glad, this moth to me
  Seems Nature's comment, clear and brief and bright,
  On man's poor dusty vanity, tonight.

1882

164

AN IRISH WILD-FLOWER

(A Barefoot Child By ___Castle)

She felt, I think, but as a wild-flower can,
  Through her bright fluttering rags, the dark, the cold.
Some farthest star, remembering what man
  Forgets, had warmed her little head with gold.

Above her, hollow-eyed, long blind to tears,
  Leaf-cloaked, a skeleton of stone arose...
O castle-shadow of a thousand years,
  Where you have fallen--is this the thing that grows?

1887

FROM AN ANCIENT MOUND

On this lone mound of legend, heaped by hands
   That have been dust from immemorial years,
Above their mythic chief, whose vassal lands
   Forget his name,--so long forgot by tears--

I dream. Below me rath and ruin are.
   England's ally there shook down Philip's fleet.
Here sings a young bird like some morning star...
   The old song's sorrow makes the new song sweet.

1893

A WORD WITH A SKYLARK

If this be all, for which I've listened long,
      Oh, spirit of the dew!
You did not sing to Shelley such a song
      As Shelley sung to you.

Yet, with this ruined Old World for a nest,
      Worm-eaten through and through--
This waste of grave-dust stamped with crown and crest--
      What better could you do?

Ah me! but when the world and I were young,
      There was an apple-tree,
There was a voice came in the dawn and sung
      The buds awake--ah me!

Oh, Lark of Europe, downward fluttering near,
      Like some spent leaf at best,
You'd never sing again if you could hear
      My Blue-Bird of the West!

1892

HIS ARGUMENT

"But if a fellow in the castle there
   Keeps doing nothing for a thousand years
And then has--everything! (That isn't fair,
   But it's--what has to be. The milk-boy hears
The talk they have about it everywhere).

"Then if the man there in the hut, you know,
   With water you could swim in on the floor,
(And it's the ground--the place is pretty, though,
   With gold flowers on the roof and half a door!)
Works--and can get no work and nothing more:

"What I will do is--nothing! Don't you see?
   Then I'll have everything, my whole life through.
But if I work, why I might always be
   Living in huts with gold flowers on them, too--
And half a door. And that won't do for me."

1887

CARRIGALINE CASTLE

(The Carman's Comments at His Own Gate on Sunday Evening)

"You must be frightened by the noise
    There at the chapel. Faith, it's only
A merrymaking. Sure, the boys
    Have been paid off. The place is lonely,
Except on Sunday, when the weather
Is fine--then they've a row together!

"You see that rye there? It's the same
    That makes the boys back there so pleasant;
Your pardon, ma'am. It is a shame
    To speak of it when you are present.
But sure, his honour should be knowing
That rye there is--our whisky, growing.

"And when they've finished up the hay
    The boys, be sure, must all be drinking;
It's what the Irish will, I say.
    No doubt his honour has been thinking
All this is wrong. A drop too many--
But then our rye's as good as any!

[Lifting his hat to the priest who drives by homeward]

"The priest, God bless him!" With a smile,
    A face as red as any rose's
He raised, and pointed slow, the while,
    To where a shattered wall encloses
A shattered stronghold, vague with distance,
Where Time has met a stout resistance.

"You see there," said he, growing grave,
    "There, do you, where that crow is flying?
One of our kings lived there--as brave
    As any. It would be worth trying

169

To find the likes of him. His name was
McCarthy!" (Ay, and here his fame was!)

"These Desmonds were a glorious race."
   (Of rebels?) Here he looked defiant
(Toward England?) Then, with kindly grace,
   Said to the child, "He was a giant."
(Ah! Master Gold-Head, you'll enchant it--
But darker things than fairies haunt it.)

"Think, will you, of an arm that reaches
   Down so that, when one's standing straight,
The hand can button the knee breeches--
   That's what they tell of him. But wait--
The buttons on them were of gold, ma'am;
At least, that's what I have been told, ma'am!"

Grim on the hill the ruin lay--
   By the still sea it dreamed and crumbled.
"Oliver Cromwell came this way,
   (In Charles's time, it was) and tumbled
The castle down!" he added, after
A little very cordial laughter.

"Oliver Cromwell knew how, well,
   To tumble old things down." "He did, ma'am,
He did," he said, as if to tell
   This strong truth pleased him. "But I'm bid, a'am,
In to my tea. --And that's it lying
Away there where the crow is flying!"

1891

170

IN THE ROUND TOWER AT CLOYNE

(C. L. P., OB. July 18, 1884)

They shivered lest the child should fall
    He did not heed a whit.
They knew it were as well to call
    To those who builded it.

"I want to climb it any way,
    And find out what is there!
There may be things--you know there may--
    Lost, in the dark somewhere."

He made a ladder of their fears
    For his light, eager feet;
It never, in its thousand years,
    Held anything so sweet.

The blue eyes peeped through dust and doubt,
    The small hands shook the Past;
"He'll find the Round Tower's secret out,"
    They, laughing, said at last.

The enchanted ivy, that had grown,
    As usual, in a night
Out of a legend, round the stone,
    He parted left and right.

And what the little climber heard
    And saw there, say who will,
Where Time sits brooding like a bird
    In that grey nest and still.

...About the Round Tower tears may fall;
    He does not heed a whit.
They know it were as well to call
    To those who builded it.

                                        1893

171

LAST OF HIS LINE

(A Young Donkey Looking through the Ruined
Window of His Family Castle)

So, there the last lord of the Castle stands
    Beside his fireless hearth,
In the wild grass of his ancestral lands--
    The saddest thing on earth.

Framed by his mullioned window, with a guard
    Of birds to circle him,
He looks into his desolate courtyard,
    Where yet the dew is dim.

The immemorial tower-rose, half awake,
    Peeps out--he looks so queer;
And old-world butterflies begin to take
    The wings of morning near.

His Norman blood shows in his long, fair ears,
    His voice, if he should--say,
Is it not like the trumpet-cry one hears
    From war-fields far away?

In his grey garments, with the ivy blown
    About his serious face,
He muses, in the sunrise bloom alone,
    On his romantic race.

(One of them, somewhere in a golden mist
    Of Shakespeare's moonlight rare,
By Queen Titania herself was kissed--
    Oh, but she thought him fair!)

His race? Great captains, poets, priests, and kings
    Were of his race, 'tis said.

The Conqueror himself-- But what odd things
    Will drift into one's head!

Look at him there among his fallen towers,
    His family tombs. Ah me,
The sweet young heir of Ruin, crowned with flowers,
    How beautiful is he!

...Take heart, my little brother! Who shall say
    What Time, the Good, will bring?
You may be king of England yet some day;
    And then--God save the King!

1891

PRO PATRIA

(From Exile)

To stand on some grey coast, uncertain, lonely,
  As some new ghost wrecked on some other world,
This is to love my country--the One only!
  To watch the boats of strange-voiced fishers, whirled
Toward islands with strange names, and then to see-
Nothing that ever was before, ah me!

To watch weird women in great cloaks, for ever
  Crying strange fruits, who will not let you be;
Or shadows in black bridal veils, who never
  On earth may hope their plighted Lord to see;
Or feel some sandal-footed, vision-eyed,
  Sad-hooded monk into your wonder glide.

More sad, to wake in some void morning, smitten
  With the sharp shadow-work of dark and dream,
Sick with a sorrow that was never written--
  No, not with heart's blood--and to hear the scream
Of the wan gulls along the hollow foam
Of alien seas--while blue-birds brood at home.

To think, if it be in the dew-dim languor
  Of the new year, of peach and apple-blooms
By the Ohio--and to start in anger,
  Almost, at glimmerings in the faery glooms
Where the primroses hide and the young thrush
Makes songs about some old-world daisy's blush.

Or, if it be when gorgeous leaves are flying,
  Through all the mighty woods, where I was born,
To sit in immemorial ruin sighing
  To braid the gold hair of the Indian corn,
With my slave-playmates singing, here and there,
Ere they were sold to their new master, Care!

Yes, if it be the time when things should wither
  In our old place--(oh, my heart, my heart!
Whence comes the evil wind that blows you whither
  It listeth?)--walking in a dream, to start
At this immortal greenness, mocking me
Alike from tower and tomb, from grass and tree:

This is to love my country! Oh, the burning
  Of her quick blood at the poor jest, the sneer,
The insolent calm question still, concerning
  Her dress, her manners! "Are you, then, so queer
At home--we mean no harm--as we have heard?"
This is to love my country, on my word!

Ah, so across the gulf they hiss and mutter:
  "Her sins they are as scarlet?" Had they been,
Whiter than wool they're washed! What of the utter
  Love of her million sons who died for sin
Not hers but theirs--who, from their common grave,
Would rise and die again were she to save!

1891

175

A SEA-GULL WOUNDED

Ah, foam-born, beautiful! So looked, I know
  The Mother of Love, when her caressing arm
Felt the stung blood stain its immortal snow,
  After the fight there on the plain ...What charm,
Of all the blind Greek gave to her, had she
That you have not--her sister of the sea?

And this young Diomed, who gave the wound
  With his first gun, if truth the bitter need
Be told (man's race is pitiless), looks round--
  His eye is used to blood--and sees you bleed...
Fly to Olympus, with your broken wing,
And Jove will laugh at you, fair, hapless thing!

1895

CONFESSION

"I love no man alive," I said, "but you,"
Upon my wedding day. Well, --that was true.
(But in the midnight moon, the midnight rain,
A mist of dead men's faces blurs the pane.)

1895

GIVING BACK THE FLOWER

So, because you chose to follow me into the subtle sadness of night,
  And to stand in the half-set moon with the weird fall-light on your
               glimmering hair
Till your presence hid all of the earth and all of the sky from my
               sight,
  And to give me a little scarlet bud, that was dying of frost, to wear,

Say, must you taunt me forever, forever? You looked at my hand
               and you knew
  That I was the slave of the Ring, while you were as free as the
               wind is free.
When I saw your corpse in your coffin, I flung back your flower to
               you;
  It was all of yours that I ever had; you must keep it, and--keep
               from me.

Ah? so God is your witness. Has God, then, no world to look after
               but ours?
  May He not have been searching for that wild star, with the trailing
               plumage that flew
Far over a part of our darkness while we were there by the freezing
               flowers,
  Or else brightening some planet's luminous rings, instead of
               thinking of you?

Or, if He was near us at all, do you think that He would sit listening
               there
  Because you sang "Hear me, Norma," to a woman in jewels and
               lace,

While, so close to us, down in another street, in the wet, unlighted
air,
There were children crying for bread and fire, and mothers who
questioned His grace.

Or perhaps He had gone to the ghastly field where the fight had been
that day,
To number the bloody stabs that were there, to look at and judge
the dead;
Or else to the place full of fever and moans where the wretched
wounded lay;
At least I do not believe that He cares to remember a word that you
said.

So take back your flower, I tell you--of its sweetness I now have no
need;
Yes, take back your flower down into the stillness and mystery to
keep;
When you wake I will take it, and God, then, perhaps will witness
indeed,
But go, now, and tell Death he must watch you, and not let you
walk in your sleep.

1867

A HUNDRED YEARS AGO

You wrong that lovely time to smile and say
  Sharp desolation shivered in the snow,
And bright sands nursed bright serpents, as today,
    A hundred years ago.

The world was full of dew and very fair,
  Before I saw it scarr'd and blacken'd so;
There was wide beauty and flush'd silence there,
    A hundred years ago.

No child's sweet grave, with rose-buds torn away
  By the most bitter winds the falls can blow,
Before my tears in freezing loneness lay
    A hundred years ago.

No phantom stars, one night in every Spring,
  Saw my faint hands, with pallor wavering slow,
Give back the glimmering fragment of a ring,
    A hundred years ago.

I did not feel this dim far-trembling doubt
  Of Christ's love in the sky, or man's below,
And hold my heart to keep one Terror out,
    A hundred years ago.

The shadow Life may wither from the grass,
  Back to God's hand the unresting seas may flow;
But what shall take me where I dream I was
    A hundred years ago?

Ah, would I care to look beyond the shine
  Of this weird-setting moon, if I could know
The peace that made my nothingness divine
    A hundred years ago?

1870

SHOULDER-RANK

"West Point?" Yes, that was the one grand argument ever so long
  At the capital, I remember now, in our far-back battle-days:
If the hour's great Leader blundered and war, therefore, went
                                  wrong,
  West Point would give a subtle faith in that great Leader's ways.

West Point--Ah, well, no doubt they can graduate generals there,
  Why, I wonder they do not send them out, plumed, sworded, and
                                ready-scarr'd,
And just because one when a boy has happened somehow to wear
  The uniform of their cadets, let his shoulders be splendidly
                                starr'd!

And if he in such starlight should grope on a little ahead
  Of the failures of two or three others and fall in some shining
                                high place,
Does that go to prove that not one in the dusty dim legions he led
  Could give him his orders in secret and point him the way to your
                                grace?

Oh, you fancy you honor where honor is due? But I feel
  You may shake the hand that finished your work, nor guess at
                              the head that planned;
What if I tell you that one, who studied the science of steel,
  In the nameless name of a Private commanded his chief to
                              command!

If I say that he passed, through a wound in his breast, up the hill,
  And lies buried where grave-marks by thousands at Arlington
                            whiten the air-
Why--you will go on and believe that our very first warrior still
  Sits smoking his pipe of Peace in the Presidential easy chair!

Published anonymously, 1871

ONE FROM THE DEAD

"Yes, yes! It is nine years, you say?
There is his portrait. He was handsome. Yes!"
His mother's mother kept her eyes away,
    But pointed up, and I could guess.

He was remembered in his room:
Of him pet window-flowers, in odors, dreamed;
His shut piano, under their sad bloom,
    The coffin of dead music seemed.

His vain-plumed hat was there; there, too,
The sword, whose bitter cause was never gained;
The coat, with glimmering shoulder-leaves, shot through
    The breast, I think, and fiercely stained.

Yet, till I saw his name--the one
His youth had soiled--above the creeping dew
Thrust high to whiten in the grave-yard sun:
    I vaguely felt, I darkly knew.

Oh, coward-praise men give to dust,
Only when it lies motionless and mute
Beneath the shining slander, which it must
    Not, till the Judgment-light, refute!

What more? If one, with voice and breath,
Had given to one a rose-geranium bud,
And changed with moons, and vanished into death
    In far-back feuds of hate and blood;

If that one, from great after-grief--
In some long, empty, lonesome cry--had said,
"I would believe; help Thou mine unbelief
    With one that was--one from the Dead;"

And felt a sudden luminous Face--
Sweet terror, yet divinest quiet, there;
And reached--to find that thorns were in the place
   Of lovely, worldly-fancied hair;

That Hands, not such as gave old flowers,
But torn with Nails, had blessed a piteous head:
That Doubt's slow question, from the unlighted hours,
   Was answered by One from the Dead;

If this had been-- You smile, and say to me,
"It were Illusion, shaped of wandering sleep!"
Well, if it were illusion, let it be:
   I have a tender Faith to keep.

1871

ANOTHER WAR

Yes, they are coming from the fort--
  Not weary they, nor dimm'd with dust;
Their march seems but a shining sport,
  Their swords too new for rust.

You think the captains look so fine,
  You like, I know, the long sharp flash,
The fair silk flag above the line,
  The pretty scarlet sash?

You like the horses when they neigh,
  You like the music most of all,
And, if they had to fight today,
  You'd like to see them fall.

I wisely think the uniform
  Was made for skeletons to wear,
But your young blood is quick and warm,
  And so--you do not care.

You lift your eager eyes and ask:
  "Could we not have another war?"
As I might give this fearful task
  To armies near and far.

Another war? Perhaps we could,
  Yet, child of mine with sunniest head,
I sometimes wonder if I would
  Bear then to see the dead!

But am I in a dream? For see,
  My pretty boy follows the men--
Surely he did not speak to me,
  Who could have spoken, then?

It was another child, less fair,
  Less young, less innocent, I know,
Who lost the light gold from its hair
  Most bitter years ago!

It was that restless, wavering child
  I call Myself. No other, dear.
Perhaps you knew it when you smiled
  Because none else was near.

Then not my boy, it seems, but I
  Would wage another war?--to see
The shining sights, to hear the cry
  Of ghastly victory?

No--for another war could bring
  No second bloom to wither'd flowers,
No second song to birds that sing
  Lost tunes in other hours!

But, friend, since time is full of pain,
  Whether men fall by field or hearth,
I want the old war back again,
  And nothing new on earth!

1872

MOCK DIAMONDS

(At the Seaside)

The handsome man there with the scar?--
  (Who bow'd to me? Yes, slightly)--
A ghastly favor of the War,
  Nor does he wear it lightly.

Such brigand-looking men as these
  Might hide behind a dagger
In--ah, "the fellow, if I please,
  With the low Southern swagger?

"One of the doubtful chivalry,
  The midnight-vengeance meetings,
Who sends, from ghostly company,
  Such fearful queer-spell'd greetings?"

No--but a soldier late to throw
  (I see not where the harm is)
Lost Cause and Conquer'd Flag below
  The dust of Northern armies.

What more? Before the South laid down
  Her insolent false glory,
He was, at this fair seaside town,
  The hero of a story.

And painted Beauty scheming through
  The glare of gilded station,
Long'd for the orange flowers--that grow
  Upon his rich plantation.

I knew him then? Well, he was young
  And I was--what he thought me;
And there were kisses hidden among
  The thin bud-scents he brought me.

One night I saw a stranger here,--
"An heiress, you must know her,"
His mother whisper'd, sliding near.
  Perhaps my heart beat lower.

The band play'd on, the hours declined,
  His eyes looked tired and dreamy;
I knew her diamonds flash'd him blind--
  He could no longer see me.

Leave your sweet jealousy unsaid:
  Your bright child's fading mother
And that guerilla from--the dead?
  Are nothing to each other.

He rose before me on the sand
  Through that vague sky's vague glimmer,
With shadows in his shadow, and
  All the dim sea grew dimmer.

He spoke? He laughed? Men hear of men
  Such words, such laughter never.
He said? "She wore Mock-Diamonds"--then,
  Pass'd to the Past forever.

                    1872

                    187

THE SORROWS OF CHARLOTTE

"The sorrows of Werther, that is the Book,
  Little girl of mine. Will I show you what
His sorrows were like? Such a brown-eyed look
  Could hardly see. Never mind, they were not
Such sorrows, I fancy, as yours or mine,
But such as in pictures look so fine,
  And such as can end--in a pistol shot.

"Is anyone else in the Book?" (I knew
  She would ask me that.) Yes, Charlotte is there.
"Then is it the Sorrows of Charlotte too?"
  No, child, for never a man would care
To write such a long sad story, you see,
As the--cutting of bread-and-butter would be;
  And never a woman had time to dare!

1872

THE GRAVE AT FRANKFORT

I turned and threw my rose upon the mound
  Beneath whose grass my old rude kinsman lies;
And thought how from his Dark and Bloody Ground
  The blood seemed in the shape of flowers to rise.

I left his dust to dew and dimness then,
  Who did not need the glitter of mock-stars
To show his wildwood generalship to men
  And light his shoulders through his border wars.

I passed his rustling wild-cane, reached the gate,
  And heard the city's noisy murmurings;
Forgot the simple hero of my State
  Looked in the gaslight, thought of other things...

Ah, that was many withered springs ago!--
  Yet once, last winter, in the whirl of snows,
Some vague half-fever, or, for aught I know,
  A wish to touch the hand that gave my rose,

Showed me a hunter of the wooded West,
  With dog and gun, beside his cabin door;
And in the strange fringed garment on his breast,
  I recognized at once the rose he wore.

1872

HER BLINDNESS IN GRIEF

What if my soul is left to me?
Oh! sweeter than my soul was he.
  Its breast broods on a coffin lid;
Its empty eyes stare at the dust.
  Tears follow tears, for treasure hid
Forevermore from moth and rust.

The sky a shadow is; how much
I long for something I can touch!
  God is a silence: could I hear
Him whisper once, "Poor child," to me!
  God is a dream, a hope, a fear,
A vision--that the seraphs see.

"Woman, why weepest thou?" One said,
To His own mother, from the dead.
  If He should come to mock me now,
Here in my utter loneliness,
  And say to me, "Why weepest thou?"
I wonder would I weep the less.

Or, could I, through these endless tears,
Look high into the lovely spheres
  And see him there--my little child--
Nursed tenderly at Mary's breast,
  Would not my sorrow be as wild?
Christ help me. Who shall say the rest?

There is no comfort anywhere.
My baby's clothes, my baby's hair,
  My baby's grave are all I know.
What could have hurt my baby? Why,
  Why did he come; why did he go?
And shall I have him by and by?

Poor grave of mine, so strange, so small,
You cover all, you cover all!
  The flush of every flower, the dew,
The bird's old song, the heart's old trust,
  The star's fair light, the darkness, too,
Are hidden in your heavy dust.

Oh! but to kiss his little feet,
And say to them, "So sweet, so sweet,"
  I would give up whatever pain
(What else is there to give, I say?)
  This wide world holds. Again, again,
I yearn to follow him away.

My cry is but a human cry.
Who grieves for angels? Do they die?
  Oh! precious hands, as still as snows,
How your white fingers hold my heart!
  Yet keep your buried buds of rose,
Though earth and Heaven are far apart.

The grief is bitter. Let me be.
He lies beneath that lonesome tree.
  I've heard the fierce rain beating there.
Night covers it with cold moonshine.
  Despair can only be despair.
God has his will. I have not mine.

1873

WORTHLESS TREASURE

If one with a sick, whispering heart should yield
  To its faint fever, brokenly, and scorn
To furrow some low, pleasant, narrow field,
  To whose sweet labor he was born;

If he should have it hold him violets
  Enough to make the fairest wreath on earth,
But with cold thanks and very dim regrets
  Refuse their humble, precious worth;

If, fiercely held by some strange gathering thought,
  Within whose doubtful darkness he could see
A thousand stars with fiery meanings caught,
  His weird and restless life should be;

If he to that great breathless night which lies
  Under the ground descended, dreaming there,
To find the fearful charm that gave his eyes
  Their glittering, ever-downward stare;

If, year by year, shut from the sun, he tried
  To gather riches from the cruel mine,
Whose slave his soul was, still to be denied
  And still to feel them shine and shine;

If, gray and ghastly, heat last should break,
  As from the dead, into the dew, and bring
Diamonds enough to light a grave, or make,
  Twice-told, the glory of a king;

If he should have his jewels cut and set,
  After some beautiful and worldly rule--
Then find himself, when in his coronet,
  Only a crowned and laughed-at Fool:

I know, today, how bitter it would be
  For him to learn his treasure was not true,
Because (as even you through love might see,)
  Because--I wear mock-jewels too!

1875

A CHILD'S PARTY

Before my cheeks were fairly dry,
  I heard my dusky playmate say:
"Well, now your mother's in the sky,
  And you can always have your way.

"Old Mistress has to stay, you know,
  And read the Bible in her room.
Let's have a party! Will you, though?"
  Ah, well, the whole world was in bloom.

"A party would be fine, and yet--
  There's no one here I can invite."
"Me and the children." "You forget--"
  "Oh, please, pretend that I am white."

I said, and think of it with shame,
  "Well, when it's over, you'll go back
There to the cabin all the same,
  And just remember you are black.

"I'll be the lady, for, you see,
  I'm pretty," I serenely said.
"The black folk say that you would be
  If--if your hair just wasn't red."

"I'm pretty anyhow, you know.
  I saw this morning that I was."
"Old Mistress says it's wicked, though,
  To keep on looking in the glass."

Our quarrel ended. At our feet
  A faint green blossoming carpet lay,
By some strange chance, divinely sweet,
  Just shaken on that gracious day.

Into the lonesome parlor we
  Glided, and from the shuddering wall
Bore, in its antique majesty,
  The gilded mirror dim and tall.

And then a woman, painted by--
  By Raphael, for all I care!
From her unhappy place on high,
  Went with us to the outside air.

Next the quaint candlesticks we took.
  Their waxen tapers every one
We lighted, to see how they'd look;
  A strange sight, surely, in the sun.

Then, with misgiving, we undid
  The secret closet by the stair--
There, with patrician dust half-hid,
  My ancestors, in china, were.

(Hush, child, this splendid tale is true!)
  Were one of these on earth today,
You'd know right well my blood was blue;
  You'd own I was not common clay.

There too, long hid from eyes of men,
  A shining sight we two did see.
Oh, there was solid silver then
  In this poor hollow world--ah me!

We spread the carpet. By a great
  Gray tree, we leant the mirror's glare,
While graven spoon and pictured plate
  Were wildly scattered here and there.

And then our table:--Thereon gleamed,
  Adorned with many an apple-bud,
Foam-frosted, dainty things that seemed
  Made of the most delicious mud.

Next came our dressing. As to that,
  I had the fairest shoes! (on each
Were four gold buttons) and a hat,
  And the plume the blushes of the peach.

But there was my dark, elfish guest
  Still standing shabby in her place.
How could I use her to show best
  My own transcendent bloom and grace?

"You'll be my grandmamma," I sighed
  After much thought, somewhat in fear.
She, joyous, to her sisters cried:
  "Call me Old Mistress! do you hear?"

About that little slave's weird face
  And rude, round form, I fastened all
My grandmamma's most awful lace
  And grandmamma's most sacred shawl.

Then one last sorrow came to me:
  "I didn't think of it before,
But at a party there should be
  One gentleman, I guess, or more."

"There's Uncle Sam, you might ask him."
  I looked, and, in an ancient chair,
Sat a bronze gray-beard, still and grim,
  On Sundays called Old Brother Blair.

Above a book his brows were bent.
  It was his pride as I had heard,
To study the New Testament
  (In which he could not spell one word).

"Oh, he is not a gentleman,"
  I said with my Caucasian scorn.
"He is," replied the African;
  "He is. He's quit a-plowing corn.

"He was so old they set him free.
  He preaches now, you ought to know.
I tell you, we are proud when he
  Eats dinner at our cabin, though."

"Well--ask him!" Lo, he raised his head.
  His voice was shaken and severe:
"Here, sisters in the church," he said,
  "Here--for old Satan's sake, come here!

"That white child's done put on her best
  Silk bonnet. (It looks like a rose.)
And this black little imp is drest
  In all Old Mistress' finest clothes.

"Come, look! They've got the parlor glass,
  And all the silver, too. Come, look!
(Such plates as these, here on the grass!)"
  And Uncle Sam shut up his book.

The priestess of the eternal flame
  That warmed our Southern kitchen hearth
Rushed out. The housemaid with her came
  Who swept the cobwebs from the earth.

Then there was one bent to the ground,
  Her hair than lilies not less white,
With a bright handkerchief was crowned:
  Her lovely face was weird as night.

I felt the flush of sudden pride,
  The others soon grew still with awe,
For, standing bravely at my side,
  My mother's nurse and mine, they saw.

"Who blamed my child?" she said. "It makes
  My heart ache when they trouble you.
Here's a whole basket full of cakes,
  And I'll come to the party too."...

Tears made of dew were in my eyes
  These after-tears are made of brine.
No sweeter soul is in the skies
  Than hers, my mother's nurse and mine.

1883

TO FRANCES CLEVELAND

Queens have been fair. One sees a radiant head
  Among the mists and shadows, here and there,
Outshine its crown. Down there among the dead,
      Ah me, queens have been fair!

Even in this world's dust and ashes yet
  I do not doubt that beauty grows and blooms.
Sometimes a living flower of it, dew-wet,
      Buds from the royal tombs.

Queens may be fair, even in the cruel sun
  Of this our day. But range them in a row:
One wears the rose of England--withering. One
      Outglitters Russia's snow.

One holds the German corn-flower. One loves best
  The Austrian edelweiss. One shows the scar
Left by the jewel-thorns of France, deep-prest--
      Forlorn as some dead star.

One hides a girl's face in Spain's widow-veil;
  One, who loves Virgil's song, has but to stir,
Or lift her gold head, and the nightingale
      Sings out his heart to her.

These, if they shine (yes, these and all the rest),
  Shine through crown-jewels and from height of place;
While you, O Lady shining in the West,
      Shine but with your own grace.

Go, if you will, among them all and stand,
  With just a mountain wild-flower in your hair,
With just the wedding-ring on your light hand
      The nation bids you wear.

Then from the Elysian Fields call Paris back:
"Say who shall have the golden apple--who?"
Though Europe, armed, should follow in his track,
He'd throw it straight to you!

1888

"SOME SWEETEST MOUTH ON EARTH..."

"Some sweetest mouth on earth bitter with brine,
   That would not kiss you back you may have kissed,
Counting your treasures by the night lamp's shrine,
   Some head that was your gold you may have missed.

Some head that glimmers down the unmeasured wave
   And makes an utter darkness where it was,
Or flung back in derision lights some grave,
   Some sudden grave cut deep into the grass.

If so, there shall be no sea there; and yet,
   Where is the soul who would not take the sea
Out of the world with it? What wild regret
   In God's high inland country there must be!

Never to lift faint eyes in love with sleep
   Across the spiritual dawn and see
Some lonesome water-bird standing dream-deep
   In mist and tide: how bitter it would be!

Never to watch the dead come sailing through
   Sunset or stars or dews of dusk or morn
With flowers shut in their folded hands that grew
   Down there in the green world where they were born.

There shall be no sea there... What shall we do?
   Shall we not gather shells, then, any more,
Or write our...names in sand, as here, we two
   Who watch the moon set on this island shore!"

before 1888

INSPIRATION AND POEM

Within the brain we feel it burn and flit
  And waver, half alighting. Say who can,
Would not the glory on the wings of it
  Strike blind the eyes of man?

We lift the eager hand, again, again,
  Dreaming to catch it. (Surely it will fly!)
And, lo! a worm, stung with freezing rain
  Of tears, crawls out to die.

1897

HAPPINESS

(A Butterfly)

Full many a maiden, in a mist of white,
  With hand that trembled toward the wedding-ring,
Thought on her threshold-rose to see you light,
    Forever-flying thing.

Full many a youth, with passionate heart astir,
  Dreaming the old divine sad dream once more
His father dreamed, joins the bright chase with her,
    And sees you flash before.

On, on forever, over bloom and dew,
  With hands thorn-torn, reached toward the eye's Desire,
Their children's children's children follow you,
    Still nigh and never nigher...

Yet, on some lily in God's Garden lit,
  You rest, perhaps. And shall we touch you there?
Not so. From height to higher height you flit,
    Still, still the soul's despair!

1897

A MISTAKE IN THE BIRD-MARKET

A Persian in the market-place
  Longed for, and so took home, a wren.
Yes, his was but a common case;
  Such always are the ways of men.

Once his, the brown bird pleased him not;
  Almost he wished it would take wing.
He loosed the cage-door, and forgot
  The dark, unsinging, lonely thing.

Night came, and touched with wind and Dew
  (Alone there in the dim moonshine)
A rose that at the window grew--
  And oh, that sudden song divine!

His children started from their sleep,
  Their Orient eyes with rapture lit'
Their pale young mother hid to weep'
  Their father did not care a whit.

He only heard the impassioned wail
  From that small prison overhead.
"My wren is but a nightingale!
  I'll wring its noisy throat!" he said.

1898

A PRAYER TO OSIRIS

(On a Sarcophagus Containing the Mummy of an Egyptian King, at
Edinburgh)

"Guide thou my barque." So run the piteous words--
  How said with faith!--upon this coffin-stone,
With the still wings of Egypt's mystic birds,
  And strange, bright, creeping creatures overgrown...
Lord of a kingdom's souls--and flocks and herds!
  You started on the lonely voyage alone!

Would no dusk daughter of your languorous land,
  No palm-tree's sister with the desert's grace,
Leave for your sake her warm world's sun and sand,
  And take beside you just a woman's place?
Or did you shake away the clinging hand,
  And shut your blind eyes on the wistful face?

You thought to land--somewhere, in golden dew,
  Where the white souls of Nile's dead lilies float.
What dark whim of your pilot-god drove you,
  O most forlorn! spite of the prayer you wrote,
To this gray isle of rock and heath, whereto
  The Scotch mist clings, dumb in your dead-man's boat?

1900

205

A SHADOWY THIRD

I

HEART AND EYES

(In His Jealous Mood)

Why, so--I can not help it, if my eyes
Must wander and alight like butterflies
To rest, one wavering instant, here or there.
One only--of the many--need you care?

Hearts have no wings wherewith to fly away.
My heart but asks beside your hearth to stay
Forever and forever. Shall it, then?
Tell me, most loved, most pitiless of men!"

II

ANOTHER WOMAN'S EYES

(In Her Jealous Mood)

"Beautiful eyes, indeed, beautiful eyes
  (He must be growing blind to think them fine!)
If on your wedding-day you had been wise,
  They might have--shed the tears you've wrung from mine.

I only wish they had. (But no, no, no.
  I'd rather weep whole seas of bitterest brine
Than let those beautiful eyes--he calls them so--
  Have one sweet tear that he has wrung from mine.)"

1903

206

A WOMAN'S "NO"

HE: "'No,' then?"
     SHE: "There is this comfort in it:
  I shall not see you growing old
And stout. Men do. But wait a minute:
  I'd like to say... the night is cold."

HE: "Why 'No?'"
     SHE: "The butterfly, in flying,
  Still wears a glory on his wing.
But catch him--if it's worth the trying--
  And he is quite another thing."

HE: "Still, 'No?'"
     SHE: "Have I not heard my mother
  Sobbing her heart out at his ways,
Because--my father, and no other,
  Was charming in his time, she says?

"It's 'No.' Because--the words of honey,
  Wherewith a lover gives a rose,
Are wormwood when one asks for money
  After one's married, I suppose."

(Aside: "It can't be that he means to leave me.)
  Just see the lightning, hear the rain.
You will be wet, and that would--grieve me."
  HE: "Good-night--and I must catch my train."

1903

THE COMING-BACK OF THE DEAD

No, not the long-pressed rose, the empty ring,
    The folded hand's cold glove,
The lonesome toy, or gold shorn hair, can bring
    Your dead to you, O Love!

They are not slaves to rise before the charms
    With which we would compel
Them to the beating breast, the yearning arms--
    I know their moods too well.

They come, they come! But never when you call.
    In their own time they start.
At hush of night, when dreams begin to fall
    Upon the half-shut heart--

Look not for them. They do not love the dark,
    Nor travel by moonlight.
They keep to their own Country till the lark
    Sings himself out of sight.

Then all at once they laugh into your face,
    Or blind you with a kiss,
Or catch you in a sudden glad embrace--
    My boy it's you!--like this!

1903

ALL IN THE BUD AND BLOOM O' THE YEAR

All in the bud and bloom o' the year,
　When the heart is sad as the first green leaf--
(Love comes not back with the rose, I fear).
　Ah, the time of joy is the time of grief--
All in the bud and bloom o' the year.

All in the bud and bloom o' the year,
　When the grass comes back, to cover the dead--
(Love comes not back with the grass, I fear;
　Does he sleep below, with a stone at his head?)--
All in the bud and bloom o' the year.

All in the bud and bloom o' the year,
　The wind keeps singing a lover's rhyme--
(Love comes not back on the wind, I fear),
　And the sweetest time is the saddest time--
All in the bud and bloom o' the year.

All in the bud and bloom o' the year,
　Heavy with honey, the bee blows by--
(Love comes not back with the bee, I fear;
　Love's sweet is bitter, Love's laugh is a cry)--
All in the bud and bloom o' the year.

All in the bud and bloom o' the year,
　When wings grow weary of alien skies--
(Love comes not back with the bird, I fear:
　Love builds no nest, save in Paradise!)--
All in the bud and bloom o' the year.

1909

A NEW THANKSGIVING

For war, plague, pestilence, flood, famine, fire,
  For Christ discrowned, for false gods set on high;
For fools, whose hands must have their heart's desire,
  We thank Thee--in the darkness--and so die.

For shipwreck: Oh, the sob of strangling seas!--
  No matter. For the snake that charms the dove;
And (is it not the bitterest of all these?)
  We thank Thee--in our blind faith--even for Love.

For breaking hearts; for all that breaks the heart;
  For Death, the one thing after all the rest,
We thank Thee, O our Father! Thou who art,
  And wast, and shalt be--knowing these are best.

1910

210

A DAFFODIL

Look!--all the vales of all the world are bright
  With you, as that of Enna was of old!
One sees the flutter of her apron light,
  All overflowing with your dew-dim gold!

Oh, shining memory of Persephone!
  Loosed from the dark of Dis, in this her time,
The sadder for its sweetness, does not she
  Out of her under-realm, rejoicing, climb?

And should the Shadow-King, in anger, miss
  His fair, young, wandering Queen, as well he might,
Then let her take the lord of Hades this--
  For his dark crown--this flower of living light!

1911

NOTES

From The Nests at Washington:

Page 37   "My Ghost"

Addressed to her cousin Kate, about whom nothing else is known. Although it moves to a conventional conclusion, the poem is remarkable for its realistic dialogue and authentic (unpoetic) details that gives, as Hanawalt states, the "sense of two real people actually talking." Such poems are not common from an era when children were portrayed in pale stereotypes.

Page 42   "To Marian Asleep"

Marian Prentice Piatt was the only daughter and the Piatt's first-born child (1862). Details of her life are sketchy: she seems to have remained in England for a time after the family's stay in Ireland, but she also lived with her parents later back in America. There is no record of her ever having married, and she died back in North Bend just a year or two before her mother.

George Prentice also wrote a poem addressed to Marian, the "infant" that bore his name. His thoroughly conventional poem, addressed to the "Child of two poets, whose rich songs/Have won a high and peerless fame," speaks of "A germ of genius, high and good/Methinks within thy bosom lies," and concludes with the wish that "May all thy life a poem be/Oh, sweet as e'er thy mother writ/And beauteous as the visions fair/That through thy father's spirit flit."

Page 44   "Hearing the Battle--July 21, 1861"

Like many inhabitants of Washington, Piatt and her husband could hear the sounds from the First Battle of Bull Run at nearby Manassas.

From <u>A Woman's Poems</u>:

Page 45   "The Fancy Ball"

An early poem in which Piatt acknowledges her dark side and states her determination to be herself, one of her main strengths as a writer. The image of the "Fancy Ball" can refer to both her life and her poetry. (See also "Shapes of a Soul," "The Order for Her Portrait," and "A Masked Ball.")

Page 46   "After Wings"

A much-anthologized poem about vanity, but also about the burden of blessing. For a modern treatment of this subject see William Stafford's "Not Having Wings" in <u>An Oregon Message</u>, p. 57.

Page 49   "Shapes of a Soul"

Piatt again rejects the "poetic" view of woman, the "pretty names for pretty moods" (<u>line 9</u>) for the honesty of the darker, "fierce," and even "viler" aspects of her nature.

Page 50   "Death before Death"

Complex poem, similar to "No Help," but in lyric form with its refrains and lonely echoes. The "her" in lines 40 and 41 seems to refer to "another sorrow" not named, but generalized into an empathic sense of tragic despair.

Page 52   "Offers for the Child"

This dialogue with mighty Atlas gives Piatt a chance to air some thoughts about current politics (referred to in <u>line 23</u> as a "quick puppet-show") while also affirming the primary importance to her of her children.

Page 55   "Her Last Gift"

Tynan's memoirs mention Piatt's being "incurably young in all her ways," though in her 50s when Tynan knew her. Old age, "the lonely mist of fall" (line 8), for the poet leads only to death, which paradoxically is the only way youth can be renewed.

Page 57   "Questions of the Hour"

Not content to write a poem only about a child's unanswerable questions, Piatt uses the "innocent reproof" about Cinderella's "mean" step-mother to turn the tables and question her own role as a mother. Line 22: Captain William Kidd was the famous pirate (c.1645-1701).

Page 61   "Playing Beggars"

Following the Civil War, many soldiers who had lost their property or their limbs were reduced to begging for a living. Piatt treats the subject in several ways (see also "Comfort through a Window," "A Neighborhood Incident," and "His Mother's Way").

Page 63   "A President at Home"

A note appended to the poem reads, "At North Bend, Ohio River--at tomb of General Harrison." The grave of General and President William Henry Harrison stands only a few hundred yards east of where the Piatts lived in North Bend.

Page 65   "Army of Occupation"

The "sleeping army" (line 6) is of the Civil War dead buried at Arlington National Cemetery across the river from Washington D.C., from where the Capitol (line 5) is clearly visible. The last stanza refers to Lincoln or to death itself.

From <u>A Voyage to the Fortunate Isles</u>:

Page 66   "There Was a Rose"

In a letter written to Edmund Stedman August 20, 1873, John James Piatt described the death of their four-day-old infant. To touch this lost rose just once again the poet is willing to travel back in time even if all the Civil War dead would have to die again. (See "No Help" and "Her Blindness in Grief.")

Page 67   "If I Were a Queen"

Stanza 2: Refers to the medieval legend of Sir Tristram (or Tristan), a knight of the round table known for his hunting prowess, who is sent to Ireland to bring back the beautiful princess Isolt (or Isolde) to be the bride of King Mark of Cornwall. Tristram and Isolt mistakenly drink a magic potion, fall in love, and ultimately die together. Wagner's famous opera about the ill-fated lovers was first performed in 1865.

Line 21: Guinevere is Arthur's beautiful, but unfaithful Queen of Camelot.

Line 22: Queen Elizabeth I (1533-1603) was known for her wardrobe (line 25) and her vanity in her appearance (line 27). The "burning" ring of Essex in line 29 refers to her favorite, Robert Devereux, 2nd earl of Essex, whom Elizabeth had executed for treason in 1601 for plotting a rebellion against her.

Stanza 4: Refers to Mary, Queen of Scots, (1542-1587). The man who died in line 34 is David Rizzio, her Italian secretary, who was murdered by assassins associated with her jealous husband, Lord Darnley. (See also "A Triumph of Travel.") Lines 38-39 allude to Mary's beheading in 1587 for her involvement in the Babington plot to assassinate Elizabeth.

Stanza 5: "She of Egypt" is Cleopatra VII (69-30 BC), the beautiful and fascinating lover of Julius Caesar and Mark Antony. After Antony killed himself with his own sword (lines 43-44), Cleopatra is said to have committed suicide by the bite of a poisonous asp (lines 41-42) she had brought to her in a basket of figs.

Lines 51-52: Boadicea (died 62 BC) was a British queen who, according to Tacitus, led an attempted revolt against the "scythed chariots" of Rome.

Lines 53-54: Vashti was the queen of King Ahasuerus of Persia, who refused to present herself to his guests ("she disobeyed/Her lord, the king in kingly wine") and was repudiated in favor of the beautiful Esther.

Lines 55-58: Solomon, King of Israel (c.960 BC), entertained the "Queen of the East, Sheba of Arabia, who was much impressed with his wisdom and wealth. However, Jesus said that Solomon in all his glory was not arrayed like the lilies of the field (Matthew 6:29).

Stanza 7: A note in A Voyage to the Fortunate Isles explains that line 62 is an "allusion to a celebrated painting of Semiramis," in which the Queen of Assyria (the legendary founder of Babylon, c.800 BC) believes her beauty will subdue the nation and make the people lie down like the lamb (see Isaiah 65:25: "The wolf and the lamb will feed together").

Lines 71-75: Penelope, the faithful wife of Ulysses, who was left behind in Ithaca to fend off many suitors during his 20-year absence. The "syrens" in line 74 refer to the sea nymphs in book xii of The Odyssey who tried to lure Ulysses with enchanting songs to shipwreck on the rocky coasts of their island.

Lines 76-79: The note published with the poem says these lines refer to Berenice's hair. Daughter of Magas, king of Cyrene, and wife of Ptolemy III Euergetes, Berenice was murdered by her son, Ptolemy IV Philopator, on his accession to the throne. Her famous hair, which she dedicated for her husband's safe return, was said to have become a constellation.

Line 81: Marie Antoinette (1755-1793), the wife of Louis XVI and Queen of France (1774-1792) who was guillotined during the French Revolution.

Line 82: Maria Theresa (1717-1780), the queen of Hungary and Bohemia, the archduchess of Austria, the wife of Francis I of the Holy Roman Empire, and the mother of Marie Antoinette.

Line 83: Blanche and Margaret were names of various queens.

Line 84: Catherine the Great (1729-1796) was the German-born empress of Russia (1762-1796).

Lines 84-86: Catherine of Aragon (1485-1536), Catholic first wife Henry VIII brought to England from Spain, was later divorced in favor of Anne Boleyn.

Lines 87-89: Catherine de Medici (1519-1589), wife of Henry II of France who died in 1559, was responsible for the massacre of the Huguenots in 1572.

Lines 91-94: Titania, the queen of fairyland (referred to in lines 95-99) and wife of Oberon in Shakespeare's Midsummer Night's Dream. In Act III, Titania is bewitched into falling in love with Bottom, the weaver, who has been given an ass's head.

Page 71   "Their Two Fortunes"

If "Annie" is Annie Boone, then it is possible that "Charlotte" is a friend of hers from New Castle, but neither speaker can be identified with any degree of certainty.

Page 72   "The Order for Her Portrait"

Line 1: Oliver Cromwell (1599-1658), Lord Protector during the Common-wealth, was known for not being vain about his appearance, and did not hide a prominent wart on his nose. The "Italian count" in line 3 was probably Lorenzo de Medici of Florence. "He of Macedon" in stanzas 4 and 5 refers to Alexander the Great (356-323 B.C.) who suffered several wounds during his military campaigns.

Page 74   "Marble or Dust?

A "Grecian Urn" poem set in a dialogue with a child in front of a statue of the recently-assassinated President Lincoln. Piatt rejects the lonely permanence of marble for the "glad pain" of temporary human life.

Page 76   "Sweetness of Bitterness"

Piatt can see the irony in her tendency to take pleasure from sadness. Stanza 5 is one of her frequent references to Cleopatra.

Page 78   "Beatrice Cenci"

In his preface to The Cenci, Shelley writes that the "portrait of Beatrice at the Colonna Palace is admirable as a work of art: it was taken by Guido during her confinement in prison." Beatrice Cenci (1577-1599) was the daughter of Francesco Cenci (1549-1598), who probably committed incest with her. She and her fellow conspirators were put to death for murdering him.

Page 79   "Over in Kentucky"

Young Sallie Bryan left her native state of Kentucky after her marriage. A note to the poem records that it was written in Cincinnati ("the smokiest city in the world" in line 1) near North Bend, Ohio, where the Piatts settled. Stanza 2 refers to her black nurse remembered from her childhood. Line 30 ends with "moon" in the Independent, but is changed to "moan" in A Voyage to the

<u>Fortunate Isles</u>. Piatt was married in 1861, the year the Civil War began.

Page 82   "Leaving Love"

Example of the way Piatt creates tension through conflicting symbolism (bloom/dust, hot/cold, North/South, statue/ life).

Page 84   "The Black Princess"

The black nurse of her childhood. The slave of the lamp in <u>line 17</u> is Aladdin's genie; the slave of the ring is a married woman. The Knight of the Pale Horse in <u>line 33</u> is death. <u>Line 39</u> refers to the Jordan River. (See "Over in Kentucky" and "A Child's Party.")

Page 86   "The Funeral of a Doll"

<u>Stanza 1</u> refers to Dickens' <u>The Old Curiosity Shop</u> (1841) with its famous scene depicting the death of the little heroine. The poem progresses from gently mocking the impersonal Victorian sentimentality accorded a child's death ("Enough to make one sorry, quite," <u>line 27</u>) to the reality of Marian's actual grief for the doll in the dark grave, which now has become personal and particular to the little girl ("See, this poor ribbon tied her hair!" <u>line 44</u>).

Page 89   "Aunt Annie"

Aunt Annie Boone, with whom Piatt lived in New Castle, Kentucky, until her marriage (<u>line 10</u>) in 1861. Piatt is holding a baby during this later visit, which makes Annie think of her own lost son.

Page 91   "The Palace-Burner"

The execution of a female "palace-burner" of the Paris Commune was pictured in the July 8, 1871, <u>Harper's Weekly</u>. Among other acts the insurrectionary government burned down the Tuileries palace. Over 17,000 of these first communists were eventually executed. Compared with these romantic figures, the poet upbraids herself for being "Languid and worldly, with a dainty need/For light and music" (lines 19-20), while keeping her soul ("she" in line 25) from expressing its "utter life," its "unappealing, beautiful despair" (lines 26-27). The dialogue with the child gives the poem a context and provides a natural progression toward her self-doubt.

Page 95   "This World"

With typical irony, Piatt proposes that we love this world almost out of pity for the many shortcomings of "her" faded old age ("the dull honey of today," line 44) that is far different from the vitality of her Greek/Roman youth.

Lines 33-34: Probably a pyramid at Gizeh, or a smaller pyramid built by a young Pharaoh of the Middle Kingdom, erected only as a monument to himself.

Line 35: The colossal statues of King Amenhotep III of Egypt near Thebes were associated in Greek mythology with Memnon, king of the Ethiopians, who came to the aid of Troy. One statue, after being partially destroyed by an earthquake in 27 BC, was said to give out musical notes at sunrise. This phenomenon was caused by the wind passing through pores in the stone as it was heated by the sun.

Lines 37-38: Refer to Greek sculpture and architecture as "toys" in the infancy of culture, as does the "playhouse pyramid" of line 34.

Lines 39-40: Mark Antony stabbed himself (through the "silken fold") out of his love for Cleopatra (see "If I Were a Queen").

Line 41: Cleopatra is "Antony's dusk queen" who had a poisonous asp brought to her in a basket of figs.

220

<u>Line 42</u>: Marcus Junius Brutus (c.85-42 BC), one of Julius Caesar's assassins, who fled Rome and committed suicide when defeated at Philippi. See Shakespeare's <u>Julius Caesar</u>.

Page 97   "A Masked Ball"

The poem catalogues a whole list of star-crossed lovers. Abelard and Heloise appear in <u>stanza 5</u>. <u>Stanza 6</u> refers to Amy Robsart (1532-1560) the wife of Robert Dudley, later Earl of Leicester, who was suspected of causing her sudden death so that he might marry Queen Elizabeth. The story is told in Sir Walter Scott's <u>Kenilworth</u>. In <u>stanza 7</u> Rowena, Rebecca, and the "saxon knight" Wilfred are all characters in Scott's <u>Ivanhoe</u>. <u>Stanzas 8 and following</u> refer to the tragic fate of Hamlet and Ophelia.

Page 99   "A Woman's Birthday"

Piatt was born on August 11th, the season referred to in <u>stanza 1</u>. This poem was written when the poet was in her thirties.

From <u>That New World</u>:

Page 100   "That New World"

The title poem from Piatt's 1876 volume, published two years after the tragic death of her oldest son, Victor. Many of the poems in the book are about death and the possibility of an after-life in "that new world."

Page 101   "The Altar at Athens"

In Acts 17:23 Paul stands on the Areopagus at Athens and addresses the people about Christianity, which he substitutes for the "unknown god" inscribed on their altar. Piatt associates this altar with all religion's attempts to implore a God beyond human definition, a God that Paul says does "not live in shrines made by human hands."

Page 102   "Lady Franklin"

Wife of Sir John Franklin (1786-1847), the British explorer who disappeared in 1847 with 128 men in northern Canada trying to find a Northwest Passage to the Pacific (lines 6-7). His frozen remains along with a diary were found in 1859.

Page 103   "Her Cross and Mine"

Piatt uses dialogue and the nun's first-person point of view to heighten the irony of this otherwise traditional sentiment.

Page 104   "Counting the Graves"

The two graves in the poem imply that Piatt had lost just one infant before the tragic death of her beloved Victor in 1874.

Page 105   "We Two"

Lines 9-10 refer to Psalm 91:5-6. Line 11 refers to Job 21:33. Line 23 is from the baptism of Christ in Matthew 3:17.

Page 107   "No Help"

In 1874, the Piatts' beloved first-born son, Victor, was tragically killed in a fireworks accident on July 4th. Hanawalt quotes an account given by Robert Stoddard in 1876 as follows: "Just at dusk as his father came home from the city, [Victor} was playing with some powder which he had stored in a bottle, when it exploded--and the same instant the little fellow ran toward them crying assuringly, 'Mamma, I am not hurt much! I am not hurt, Mamma!' But the next moment he was no longer with them." (See "Her Blindness in Grief.")

Page 108   "Asking for Tears"

Tears for Piatt are often the only consolation for women, and are life-giving in the dry sandy desert of grief.

Page 110   "Tradition of Conquest"

About the Duke of Marlborough, John Churchill (1650-1722), British general and statesman who defeated the French at Blenheim in Bavaria on August 13, 1704. As a reward, Blenheim Palace was built for him at government expense near Oxford. His Duchess, Sarah Jennings, was often difficult and eventually caused his fall from grace with Queen Anne in 1711.

Page 111   "A Dead Man's Friends"

Stanza 3 refers to a Titian (1477-1576) painting of Venus, the Roman deity associated with Aphrodite, the Greek goddess of love. The painting was probably "Venus Anadyomene," (1519/1525) in the National Gallery of Scotland, Edinburgh, in which Venus is leaning forward with her dark hair held in both hands.

Page 113   "The Little Boy I Dreamed About"

The innocence of childhood inevitably disappears into a dream (stanza 1), fairyland (stanza 8), or is equated with death (stanza 9). Yet the tone remains playful, and the examples of mischief ring true, anchoring the poem in reality. (See also "My Babes in the Wood" and "The Baby's Brother.")

Page 116   "More about Fairies"

The Snake in the Garden in stanza 3 signifies the loss of simple faith. The tightly-woven discussion of fairies and the Bible foreshadows the final movement to the "we children" in line 28, signifying the universal loss of innocence that no one can escape. Other loss of innocence poems include "The Witch in the Glass" and "The Sad Story of a Little Girl."

223

From Dramatic Persons and Moods:

Page 121   "A Pique at Parting"

Between 1870 and 1876, when John James was again employed in Washington, Sarah and her several small children spent the summers apart from him back home in North Bend.

Page 123   "The Descent of the Angel"

The reality of marriage after the romance of courtship. One of Piatt's many dark poems about marriage. However, she also wrote many others which view marriage positively or even playfully.

Page 124   "Her Word of Reproach"

The reproach is to her husband for being content to state love in simple platitudes (line 8) when to the poet death is very real (line 14) and life beyond the grave unsure. Yet the stark uncertainty of human life, the "passion of human pain" (line 22) gives love its poignancy, and for Piatt a deep human necessity that her husband takes too lightly.

Page 125   "Caprice at Home"

Piatt indulges in a bit of self-deprecating laughter at her tendency to become too morbid. "Some one some one loves" (line 17) and "wrong and wrong and wrong" (line 26) echo "the bell" in line 16.

Page 127   "A Ghost at the Opera"

See "Giving Back the Flower."

Page 129   "A Lesson in a Picture"

See "The Descent of the Angel."

Page 131   "After the Quarrel"

Line 41: Raphael, the Italian painter (1483-1520), is an archetypal romantic figure that Piatt uses in several poems.

Page 139   "A Hint of Homer" (Their Heroic Lesson)

According to a note published with the poem, the events from The Iliad and The Odyssey mentioned here resulted from Piatt's reading her children Stories from Homer by Rev. Alfred J. Church. First published with this title in Wide-Awake in December 1878, the poem appears with the title "A Hint from Homer" in Dramatic Persons and Moods (1880), even though listed in the table of contents as "A Hint of Homer." It is reprinted in The Witch in the Glass (1889) under the title "Their Heroic Lesson."

From An Irish Garland:

Page 140   "In Clonmel Parish Churchyard"

First published under the title "At the Grave of Charles Wolfe." Wolfe was the young rector at Donaghmore (1818-1821) who had written "The Burial of Sir John Moore," which contains the words "Not a drum was heard," (lines 15-16). Inspired by Southey's account of Moore's death at Corunna, Wolfe's famous short elegy had appeared in the Newry Telegraph in 1817 and was discovered by Byron five years later. Wolfe died of tuberculosis in 1823. A note in An Enchanted Castle, very likely written (as were most of the notations about her poems) by her husband John James, states that "Queenstown, Ireland, formerly called the Cove of Cork, of which Clonmel Parish Churchyard is the cemetery, was early a place of resort for consumptives."

Also interesting, and characteristic of Piatt, is her later account of visiting Wolfe's grave in her essay "An Old Seaport Graveyard" in The Hesperian Tree, volume 2 (1903): "Since then, by the way, I have been pained to learn, from the evidence of the clergyman who read the last service, that Sir John Moore was not buried 'By the struggling moonbeam's misty light and the lantern dimly burning,' which was the most poetical thing that ever happened--I mean that ever did not happen--to him, but in the plain, honest presence of the sun. I prefer Charles Wolfe's version of the story."

Page 141   "A Call on Sir Walter Raleigh"

Raleigh, for his services to Queen Elizabeth I, was granted 42,000 acres of land in the counties of Cork and Waterford, which included the town of Youghal. He was appointed mayor, 1588-89, and lived for a while at Myrtle Grove, a gabled house in private grounds just north of St. Mary's Church. The note in An Enchanted Castle in reference to line 33 states: "St. Mary's Church, one of the most ancient and interesting, from an historical point of view, among old Irish churches, almost adjoins the house known as Sir Walter Raleigh's at Youghal, County Cork, Ireland." The Oxford Literary Guide to the British Isles mentions it "is possible that Spenser, who had been writing The Faerie Queene at [nearby] Kilcolman, visited Raleigh here and discussed the poem with him."

Page 143   "A Child's Cry"

Subtitled "At Kilcolman Castle, March 1883," the poem refers to a child who died (Spenser's?) when the castle was set on fire. This moves Piatt far more deeply than the books of The Faerie Queene ("perhaps almost too long") that Spenser wrote at the castle. The castle, near Doneraile, Cork, was part of the 3,000-acre estate granted to Spenser after the crushing of the Desmond rebellion in 1586. After his marriage to Elizabeth Boyle in 1594, Spenser was back at the castle by 1596, but was forced to leave when his home was attacked and burned.

From <u>The Children Out-of Doors</u>:

Page 145   "The Thought of Astyanax beside Iulus"

An extensive note in <u>The Children Out-of-Doors</u> reads in part: "The pathetic little episode to which this piece refers is related in the third book of Virgil's <u>Aeneid</u>, lines 482-492, where the poet describes Aeneas meeting Andromache during his wanderings, after the fall of Troy, with his son Ascanius (also called Iulus). To the latter Andromache gives some garments wrought by herself, and in presenting them she recalls her own boy Astyanax, who, in obedience to an oracle, had been thrown headlong from the walls of the Trojan city and killed. This was after the death of Hector, his father, whose parting with Andromache--in which the child 'headed like a star,' together with 'the horse-hair plume,' is mentioned--forms one of the most famous passages in the <u>Iliad</u> of Homer." In translation, Virgil's description concludes: "Just such eyes, just such hands, just such features he had, and he would now be growing up in equal age with thee."

Piatt's deep empathy with other women who have lost a child (<u>line 30</u>: "Her grief is more than I can bear.") is also seen in "Aunt Annie" (as in <u>line 52</u>: "I almost heard her own heart beat.").

Page 148   "His Mother's Way"

Piatt notes the poem was written after reading newspaper accounts about the treatment of the "tramp." (See "Playing Beggars" and "A Neighborhood Incident.")

Page 150   "In Street and Garden" (I)

The child's literal faith affirms the heaven that he can actually "see," as opposed to the rumored hell that cannot be found by digging in the earth. (See also "Calling the Dead" and "Child's-Faith.")

Page 151   "The Christening"

The "spinning-wheel" and "spindle" in Stanza 2 refer to the
activities of the Fates.

From In Primrose Time:

Page 152   "A Portrait at Youghal"

Another note in An Enchanted Castle records that this poem
was written "After previously visiting the house of Sir Walter
Raleigh. Youghal is pronounced very much like 'yawl.'" Piatt
seems to treat both Raleigh's romanticism and Youghal's local pride
with mild irony, and these events are described more fully in her
essay "A Sunday at Youghal" in The Hesperian Tree (1900).

Page 153   "Two Innocents Abroad"

This poem, occasioned by the events "On Coronation Day,
June 1884," shows Piatt's thoughts on monarchy framed in a
dialogue between two of her "innocent" children. The title and the
tone reflect her reading of Twain. The six-year-old is her youngest
son Cecil, and the older child may have been Louis, who drowned
that same summer. General Charles George Gordon (last stanza),
the romantic British officer who fought in Asia and Africa, was in
the Sudan in 1884, and would die in the siege of Khartoum in
January 1885. Tennyson wrote his memorial that is in Westminster
Abbey.

From The Witch in the Glass:

Page 156   "The Sermon of a Statue"

In the Poet's Corner of Westminster Abbey, Piatt's young
son wants to hear the "sermon" of the "marble men" instead of the
live sermon being given in the church (lines 12-13). Shakespeare is
the "peerless man" (line 15) who delivers the silent sermon from "his

228

text" (line 16). The poem contains Shakespeare's "jesters," "globe," and other references in this "sermon in stone".

Page 157   "After Her First Party"

Dialogue poem that shows Piatt's remarkable gift for genuine conversation packed in tightly-structured stanzas.

Page 159   "A Triumph of Travel"

Mentions the familiar attractions after a visit to Edinburgh, including Holyrood where the "bluid" (line 26) of the unfortunate Rizzio was shed.

Page 160   "The Story of a Storm"

The storm in the poem has provided an excuse for the two brothers to reconcile after an argument about Hector, the Trojan hero, son of Priam, who was slain by Achilles in Homer's The Iliad.

Page 161   "The Coming Out of Her Doll"

As the empathic young girl, Marian, dresses up her doll "Rose" for a graduation, she feels grown up herself. Note line 10: "Papa, he always comes home late and tired."

Page 163   "At the Grave of a Suicide"

It was customary to bury suicides in a separate area outside "consecrated" burial grounds.

Page 164   "The Night-Moth's Comment"

Fourth Earl of Chesterfield, Philip Dormer Stanhope (1694-1773), was an English statesman and noted letter-writer on manners and society.

From <u>An Irish Wild-Flower</u>:

Page 166   "From an Ancient Mound"

Philip's fleet in <u>line 6</u> refers to the Spanish Armada of 130 ships defeated by the British navy in 1588.

Page 167   "A Word with a Skylark"

Perhaps the most anthologized of Piatt's poems, it was sometimes printed with the subtitle "A Caprice of Homesickness." After her early infatuation with Byron, Piatt admired the work of Shelley second only to that of Shakespeare.

Page 169   "Carrigaline Castle"

Piatt's interest in this castle reduced to ruin in the mid-17th century shows not only her fascination with history, but also her ability to convey the dialect and humor of the "carman" in a dramatic monologue.

Page 171   "In the Round Tower at Cloyne"

The poem singled out for praise by Yeats in his <u>Speaker</u> review of July 1893. The subtitle refers to her son who drowned July 18, 1884.

Page 172   "Last of His Line"

Piatt's rather broad lampoon of the long line of Norman kings. She was no doubt familiar with Coleridge's "To a Young Ass." Other poems of hers, as in <u>stanza 6</u> here, also make reference to the scene in <u>A Midsummer Night's Dream</u> (see "If I Were a Queen"). A footnote after "England" in the next-to-last line reads "In America we should say President of the United States."

In this complex poem, subtitled "From Exile," Piatt explores her feelings about America after several years' absence in Ireland.

From A Child's World Ballads:

Page 176   "A Sea-Gull Wounded"

In The Iliad, Diomedes (line 7) wounds Prince Aeneas, whose mother is Aphrodite (Venus), "foam born" (line 1) "Mother of Love" (line 2). As the goddess rushed to the battlefield to save her son, Diomedes wounded her arm (lines 2-4 and 7-10). Letting go of Aeneas, she flies to Olympus where Zeus laughed at her (lines 11-12) and told her to stay away from battle and confine herself to the domain of love. The seagull seems to be the white dove sacred to Aphrodite.

Uncollected Poems from Periodicals:

Page 178   "Giving Back the Flower"

Line 14: From Vincenzo Bellini's (1801-1835) opera Norma (1832), in which the heroine has a secret relationship with a Roman proconsul.

Page 184   "Another War"

Piatt identifies with her son's innocent, romantic view of war, perhaps referring to the first years of her marriage in Washington when so many soldiers were leaving for what they thought would be a glorious and romantic war, before the grim reality of the Civil War deprived them and the poet of their youthful innocence.

Page 186   "Mock Diamonds"

At a seaside resort the narrator is questioned about her relationship with other men there. The false romance with the Southern "brigand" turned out to be a mock diamond, like the non-existent fortune of the "heiress" he pursued.

Page 188   "The Sorrows of Charlotte"

Line 1 is a reference to Goethe's The Sorrows of Werther (1774).

Page 189   "The Grave at Frankfort"

Her "kinsman" (line 2) was Daniel Boone (1735-1820), the "hero of my State" from whom Piatt (Sarah Morgan Bryan) was descended. Piatt's note: "General Boone, backwoodsman of Kentucky--Byron." The rose carries several meanings: romance, the war, a wound, and death (see "Giving Back the Flower").

Page 190   "Her Blindness in Grief"

Line 13 Jesus spoke to Mary at the resurrection on Easter morning.

Page 194   "A Child's Party"

Dialogue between a white child and her slave playmate. The Old Mistress is the grandmother who owns the plantation. Line 45: Bennett cites an 1886 letter in which Piatt verifies that this incident from her childhood occurred as described in the poem. The cook and Brother Blair would have had authority over the child, who is rescued by her beloved black nurse.

Page 199   "To Frances Cleveland"

On June 2, 1886, President Cleveland, near 50, married beautiful, young Frances Folsom, age 22. The marriage turned out happily, and Frances Cleveland was wildly popular. Stanza 8:

Paris, son of King Priam of Troy, was asked to award the golden apple, which he gave to Aphrodite for promising him the most beautiful woman in the world. Piatt wrote this poem while in Ireland.

Page 201   "Some Sweetest Mouth on Earth..."

Quoted in Katharine Tynan's Twenty-Five Years: Reminiscences in 1913, in which she talks about Piatt's love for the sea, especially at dawn. Tynan recalls that in this, "one of the most beautiful of her poems, I see her dear beloved little soul plain." Piatt's grief for her drowned son is also apparent in the poem. (See note on "Her Last Gift.")

Page 204   "A Mistake in the Bird-Market"

A Oriental fable popular in the nineteenth century told of a nightingale that fell in love with a rose. The Persian's rage is because the bird sings to the rose instead of to him.

Page 205   "A Prayer to Osiris"

Osiris, husband and brother of Isis, was the ancient Egyptian god of the underworld and judge of the dead. The prayer in line 1 ("Guide thou my barque") comes as an ironic conclusion for Piatt who found the sarcophagus and its inscription in the northern mists (lines 17-18) of Edinburgh.

Page 209   "All in the Bud and Bloom o' the Year"

Piatt did not publish many purely lyrical poems, but songs like this attest to her skill in writing them.

Page 210   "A New Thanksgiving"

An ironic, bitter prayer of thanksgiving. One of Piatt's darker poems.

This poem, written when Piatt was in her seventies, is perhaps the most beautiful of the few purely lyric poems she wrote. Persephone (line 5), daughter of Demeter and maiden of springtime, was lured to her capture by the Shadow-King (line 9) of the underworld (Hades) while she was gathering flowers in the vale of Enna, a city in Sicily where the abduction supposedly took place (line 2). This myth of the seasons carries an inherent sadness (line 7) because of the transitory nature of youth and beauty. Stanza 2 also refers obliquely to the poet's own advanced age. (See also "All in the Bud and Bloom o' the Year.")

BIBLIOGRAPHY OF PUBLICATIONS BY SARAH PIATT INCLUDING REVIEWS

Books by Sarah Piatt:

A Woman's Poems. Boston: James R. Osgood & Co., 1871. Issued anonymously. Printed 18 of the 22 poems from The Nests at Washington along with 37 new poems.

A Voyage to the Fortunate Isles. Boston: James R. Osgood & Co., 1874, 1885. By Mrs. S.M.B. Piatt. 51 new poems.

That New World and Other Poems. Boston: Houghton, Mifflin Co., 1877. 43 poems, including several "with children."

Poems in Company with Children. Boston: Houghton, Mifflin Co., [1877]. Collects 53 poems, most of which appeared in earlier books. Issued as A Book about Baby and Other Poems. Boston, 1882. At University of Kentucky.

Dramatic Persons and Moods with Other Poems. Boston: Houghton, Mifflin Co., 1880. 49 poems, including 10 "double quatrains," and 17 poems with children.

An Irish Garland. Edinburgh: 1884. Boston & New York: Houghton, Mifflin Co., 1885. Six Irish poems along with "miscellaneous" others. By Sarah M.B. Piatt.

Selected Poems: A Voyage to the Fortunate Isles and Other Poems. London: Kegan Paul, Trench & Co., 1885. Boston & New York: Houghton, Mifflin Co., 1886.

Songs and Satires. Boston: 1886.

In Primrose Time. London: Kegan Paul, Trench & Co., 1886. Boston & New York: Houghton, Mifflin Co., 1886. 12 Irish poems.

Child's-World Ballads. Sub-titled Three Little Emigrants: A Romance of Cork Harbour, 1884. Cincinnati: Robert Clarke, 1887.

The Witch in the Glass. Boston: Houghton, Mifflin Co., 1889. 49 poems & notes.

An Irish Wild-Flower. New York: Frederick Stokes, 1891.

An Enchanted Castle. London: Longmans, Green & Co., 1893. 30 poems including all 12 from In Primrose Time.

Poems. London & New York: Longmans, Green, 1894. Two Vols.

Child's-World Ballads. Second Series. Westminster: A. Constable, 1895.

The Gift of Tears. Cincinnati: Western Literary, 1906. Small booklet.

Books by Both Piatts:

The Nests at Washington. New York: Walter Low, 1864. London: Sampson Low, Son   & Co., 1864. Contains 22 poems by Sarah following 44 poems by her husband John James Piatt.

The Children Out-of-Doors. Cincinnati: Robert Clarke & Co., 1885. Published anonymously by "Two in One House." Contains eight poems by John James in Section I, eight by Sarah in Section II, and a concluding poem by John James.

Magazine Publications by Sarah Piatt:

"The Fancy Ball." Galaxy 1 (June 15, 1866): 372. Reprinted in the Mac-A-Cheek Press (August 10, 1866): 348.

"Shapes of a Soul." Galaxy 3 (January 15, 1867): 196.

"Giving Back the Flower." Galaxy 3 (February 1867): 409.

"A Sister of Mercy." Galaxy 7 (April 1869): 568.

"To-Day." Atlantic Monthly 23 (April 1869): 513.

"A Lily of the Nile." Galaxy 7 (May 1869): 733-734.

"A Statue." Atlantic Monthly 24 (July 1869): 25.

"A Woman's Last Gift." Galaxy 8 (July 1869): 100.

"A Child's First Sight of Snow." Galaxy 9 (January 1870): 93.

"A Hundred Years Ago." Galaxy 9 (February 1870): 238.

"Playing Beggars." Galaxy 10 (October 1870): 509-510.

"My Artist." Overland Monthly 5,4 (October 1870): 344-345.

"My Babes in the Wood." Harper's Monthly 41 (November 1870): 825.

"Offers for the Child." Overland Monthly 6,3 (March 1871): 286.

"After Wings." Independent 23 (March 2, 1871): 8.

"The Highest Mountain." Independent 23 (March 23, 1871): 6.

"My Dead Fairies." Independent 23 (May 18, 1871): 6.

"The Clothes of a Ghost." Scribner's Monthly 11 (June 1871): 204-205.

"Our Lost Picture." Independent 23 (June 29, 1871): 2.

"Beatrice Cenci." Overland Monthly 7,1 (July 1871): 68.

"A Life in a Mirror." Independent 23 (July 27, 1871): 1.

"One from the Dead." Overland Monthly 7,3 (September 1871): 224.

"Marble or Dust?" Atlantic Monthly 28 (October 1871): 414.

"A Child's City." Independent 23 (October 5, 1871): 4. Reprinted in The Capital (January 5, 1873): 1.

"Thorns." Independent 23 (November 2, 1871): 8.

"Our Buried Bird." Independent 23 (December 14, 1871): 1.

"Silence." Independent 24 (January 11, 1872): 2.

"There Was a Rose." Atlantic Monthly 29 (February 1872): 139.

"Over in Kentucky." Independent 24 (February 1872): 2. Reprinted in The Capital   (May 10, 1874): 6.

"Sometime." Independent 24 (February 29, 1872): 1. Reprinted in The Capital (May 24, 1874): 6.

"A Precious Seeing." Independent 24 (March 7, 1872): 10.

"A Well-Known Story." Independent 24 (May 2, 1872): 8.

"To-Morrow." Independent 24 (June 6, 1872): 8.

"The Order for Her Portrait." Independent 24 (July 4, 1872): 4.

"If I Were a Queen." Independent 24 (July 18, 1872): 1. Reprinted in The Capital (April 19, 1874): 7.

"Leaving Love." Independent 24 (September 5, 1872): 8.

"Why Should We Care?" Independent 24 (October 17, 1872): 2.

"Love-Stories." Independent 24 (October 31, 1872): 2.

"The Palace-Burner." Independent 24 (November 28, 1872): 2.

"The Black Princess." Independent 24 (December 26, 1872): 2.

"One Little Bird." Independent 25 (February 13, 1873): 196.

"This World." Independent 25 (May 22, 1873): 644.

"The Play." Independent 25 (July 17, 1873): 894.

"A Voyage to the Fortunate Isles." Harper's Monthly 47 (August 1873): 452-453.

"His Fairy Godmother." Independent 25 (August 21, 1873): 1086.

"A Doubt." Independent 25 (November 6, 1873): 1378.

"Her Blindness in Grief." Independent 25 (November 20, 1873): 1303.

"A Very Old Grave." Galaxy 16 (December 1873): 832. Reprinted in The Capital (April 25, 1875): 6.

"A Prettier Book." Independent 26 (April 30, 1874): 4.

"Life or Love." Appleton's 11 (May 23, 1874): 658-659.

"Unheeded Gifts." Independent 26 (July 16, 1874): 4.

"When the World Was Full of Snow." Appleton's 12 (July 25, 1874): 107.

"Two Veils." Atlantic Monthly 34 (August 1874): 215.

"We Two." Independent 26 (September 10, 1874): 7.

"Counsel--In the South." Galaxy 18 (November 1874): 659.

"Making Peace." Scribner's Monthly 9 (November 1874): 31.

"From Two Windows." Galaxy 18 (December 1874): 838.

"Enchanted." Atlantic Monthly 35 (January 1875): 74

"Comfort." Galaxy 19 (February 1875): 169.

"Her Triumph at Last." Galaxy 19 (March 1875): 324.

"Calling the Dead." Atlantic Monthly 35 (April 1875): 395. Reprinted in The Capital (December 17, 1876): 2.

"Folded Hands." Atlantic Monthly 35 (June 1875): 670.

"The Altar at Athens." Independent 27 June 10, 1875): 4.

"The Longest Death Watch." Atlantic Monthly 36 (August 1875): 140-142.

"The Gift of Empty Hands." Harper's Monthly 51 (August 1875): 437.

"Answering a Child." Independent 27 (September 30, 1875): 4.

"Her Lover's Trial." Galaxy 20 (October 1875): 508.

"That New World." Atlantic Monthly 36 (October 1875): 426-427.

"Counting the Graves." Appleton's 14 (November 27, 1875): 692.

"Comfort--By a Coffin." <u>Scribner's Monthly</u> 11 (January 1876): 366.

"The Dead Connoisseur's Friends." <u>Atlantic Monthly</u> 37 (January 1876): 24. Published in <u>That New World</u> as "A Dead Man's Friends."

"Her Cross and Mine." <u>Independent</u> 28 (January 27, 1876): 4.

"Tradition of Conquest." <u>Galaxy</u> 21 (February 1876): 218.

"Sad Wisdom--Four Years Old." <u>Appleton's Journal</u> 15 (March 11, 1876): 340. Reprinted in <u>The Capital</u> (March 19, 1876): 2.

"My Birthright." <u>Scribner's Monthly</u> 12 (May 1876): 119.

"The King's Memento Mori." <u>Atlantic Monthly</u> 38 (July 1876): 71.

"In a Queen's Domain." <u>Independent</u> 28 (July 13, 1876): 7.

"The Bird in the Brain." <u>Atlantic Monthly</u> 38 (August 1876): 202.

"Giving Up the World." <u>Atlantic Monthly</u> 38 (October 1876): 417. Reprinted in <u>The Capital</u> (January 7, 1877): 6.

"Two in Two Worlds." <u>Appleton's</u> 2 (January 1877): 88.

"The House Below the Hill." <u>Atlantic Monthly</u> 39 (February 1877): 223-225.

"In Weariness." <u>Appleton's</u> 2 (March 1877): 246.

"The Happier Gift." <u>Atlantic Monthly</u> 39 (April 1877): 482.

"Child's-Faith." <u>Scribner's Monthly</u> 14 (June 1877): 247.

"Caprice at Home." <u>Appleton's</u> 3 (July 1877): 67.

"Lie Still!" (Requiescat) <u>Potter's American Monthly</u> 9 (July 1877): 40.

"A Ghost." <u>Atlantic Monthly</u> 40 (August 1877): 187.

"To Be Dead." <u>Appleton's</u> 3 (September 1877): 205.

"Into the World and Out." <u>Scribner's Monthly</u> 14 (September 1877): 636.

"For Another." <u>Lippincott's</u> 20 (October 1877): 405.

"Presentiment." <u>Potter's American Monthly</u> 9 (October 1877): 303.

"Ah, Chasms and Cliffs of Snow." <u>Atlantic Monthly</u> 40 (November 1877): 547-548.

"A Look into the Grave." <u>Appleton's</u> 4 (January 1878): 31.

"In Doubt." <u>Appleton's</u> 4 (February 1878): 104.

"After the Quarrel." <u>Scribner's Monthly</u> 16 (June 1878): 274-275.

"Spring-Song." <u>Atlantic Monthly</u> 41 (June 1878): 790.

"Their Heroic Lesson." <u>Wide-Awake</u> (December 1878): 359.

"A Flower in a Book." <u>Atlantic Monthly</u> 42 (December 1878): 768.

"One Out-of-Doors." <u>Atlantic Monthly</u> 42 (December 1878): 682-683.

"Three Songs." <u>Atlantic Monthly</u> 43 (February 1879): 183-184.

"The Descent of the Angel." <u>Scribner's Monthly</u> 18 (May 1879): 111.

"Her Reproof to a Rose." <u>Scribner's Monthly</u> 18 (June 1879): 233. Published in <u>Dramatic Persons and Moods</u> as "Reproof to a Rose."

"A Lesson in a Picture." <u>Atlantic Monthly</u> 44 (September 1879): 369-370.

"Transfigured." <u>Scribner's Monthly</u> 19 (December 1879): 195.

"His Mother's Way." <u>Independent</u> 32 (February 5, 1880): 26.

"Watching the Cows." <u>Scribner's Monthly</u> 20 (June 1880): 280.

"The Thought of Astyanax Beside Iulus." <u>Scribner's Monthly</u> 21 (November 1880): 77.

"My Neighbor's Confession." <u>Scribner's Monthly</u> 21 (January 1881): 415.

"Two Visitors of Fairy-Land." <u>St. Nicholas</u> 8 (February 1881): 277.

"The Witch in the Glass." <u>Scribner's Monthly</u> 21 (March 1881): 744.

"The Years." <u>Independent</u> 33 (April 7, 1881): 1.

"A Neighborhood Incident." <u>Independent</u> 33 (August 11, 1881): 1.

"My Neighbor's Ring." <u>Atlantic Monthly</u> 48 (October 1881): 517.

"The Night-Moth's Comment." <u>Atlantic Monthly</u> 49 (June 1882): 818.

"It Is Not Yesterday." <u>Century</u> 24 (October 1882): 938.

"A Call on Sir Walter Raleigh." <u>Atlantic Monthly</u> 51 (June 1883): 758-759.

"The Gift of Tears." <u>Atlantic Monthly</u> 52 (August 1883): 232.

"A Portrait at Youghal." Manhattan 2 (September 1883): 289.

"A Child's Party." Wide-Awake 17 (October 1883): 1.

"At the Grave of Charles Wolfe." Century 27 (December 1883): 304.

"One Happy Woman." Manhattan 2 (December 1883): 584.

"Birds at Monkstown Castle." St. Nicholas 11 (December 1883): 105-106.

"The Christening." Atlantic Monthly 53 (June 1884): 779.

Poem in Salmagundi. Manhattan 4 (July 1884): 124.

"In Primrose Time." St. Nicholas (May 1885): 497-498.

Poems. Irish Monthly 14 (1886): 381. Piatt published many poems in the Irish Monthly between 1884-1895.

"At the Grave of a Suicide." Atlantic Monthly 58 (July 1886): 76.

"The Sermon of a Statue." Century 32 (September 1886): 715.

"From An Ancient Irish Mound." Century 34 (May 1887): 53.

"An Irish Wild-Flower." Scribner's 1 (May 1887): 593. Reprinted in Atheneum 99 (January 2, 1892): 13, and in Nation 54 (March 31, 1892): 254.

"A Coin of Lesbos." Lippincott's 39 (June 1887): 998. Reprinted in Lippincott's 94 (September 1914): 323.

"His Argument." Century 34 (October 1887): 880.

"The Night Cometh." Lippincott's 41 (February 1888): 241.

"To Frances Cleveland." Belford's 1,2 (July 1888): 187.

"When Saw We Thee?" Belford's 1,5 (October 1888): 663.

"Queen's Epitaph." Belford's (March 1889): n.p.

"Dance of the Daisies." St. Nicholas 16 (August 1889): 731.

"Child's World." Living Age 184 (January 25, 1890): 239.

"Shadow-Bird and His Shadow." St. Nicholas 17 (February 1890): 335-336.

"Seven Little Indian Stars." St. Nicholas 17 (March 1890): 406.

"A Word with a Skylark." Atheneum 99 (January 2, 1892): 14. Reprinted in Critic 24 (February 24, 1894): 122.

"Echo and Narcissus." Cosmopolitan 12 (April 1892): 732.

"Woman's Last Word." Spectator (London) 77 (October 3, 1896): 441.

"A Wood-Bird's Whim." Century 53 (January 1897): 423.

"A Dance of Daisies (In Ireland)." Independent 49 (June 24, 1897): 801.

"Inspiration and Poem." Bookman 5 (July 1897): 410. Reprinted in Bookman 30 (January 1910): 470.

"Happiness (A Butterfly)." Harper's Monthly 96 (December 1897): 39-40.

"Our First Christmas in Ireland." (Prose) Independent 49 (December 23, 1897): 1677-1678. Prose sketch.

"An Old Year's Diary." New England Magazine 17 (January 1898): 532.

"The Sweetest Singer." Scribner's Monthly 23 (April 1898): 447-448.

"A Mistake in the Bird-Market." Century 56 (October 1898): 835.

"If I Remember You." Century 57 (December 1898): 178.

"Heart's-Ease Over Henry Heine." Harper's Monthly 98 (March 1899): 523.

"The Sermon of a Robin." Independent 51 (June 8, 1899): 1535.

"The Swan of Avon." Harper's Monthly 101 (October 1900): 711.

"A Handful of Grass on Victor Hugo's Coffin." Harper's Monthly 101 (November 1900): 923.

"Old Portraits." St. Nicholas 30 (January 1903): 252-253.

"Her Assurance (After Shipwreck)." Independent 55 (October 8, 1903): 2406.

"Poet and Sexton." Century 68 (June 1904): 326.

"One Poet Dead." Independent 56 (June 2, 1904): 1248.

"A Cuckoo's Call." Scribner's Monthly 43 (March 1908): 282.

"All in the Bud and Bloom o' the Year." Harper's Monthly 119 (October 1909): 726.

"A New Thanksgiving." Independent 69 (November 24, 1910): 1128.

"A Bird Without A Mate." Independent 70 (January 5, 1911): 37.

"A Daffodil." Independent 70 (May 25, 1911): 1112.

Newspaper Publications by Sarah Piatt:

Many of Piatt's earliest poems were published in the Louisville Journal, edited by George D. Prentice. A few other early poems appeared in the Galveston News, and the New York Ledger. The following poems were all published in the Louisville Journal before her marriage to John James Piatt in June 1861 under her initials "S. M. B." or (later) "by Sallie M. Bryan" from Newcastle, Ky. They represent her apprentice work and are not included in this volume.

Poems in the Louisville Journal:

"Nobility and Ignobility of Queen Elizabeth." September 13, 1855. Prentice explains that this poem by "Miss Sarah Bryan" was assigned as exercise to be read at an exhibition by a member of the graduating class of Rev. Sumner's Female Seminary at Newcastle.

"To An Estranged Friend." S.M.B. November 12, 1855. Prentice adds this "young poetess writes well, and we are told she not only hates flattery but dislikes just praise."

"Thoughts for Departed Autumn." December 13, 1855.

"The Mourner in the Festive Hall." January 5, 1856. Prentice writes, "Mark our prediction now. It is that the young Kentucky girl, who wrote the following and who has written several kindred poems for our column, will win a name that our generation will love to cherish."

"The Spirit's Return." January 21, 1856. Prentice describes her "spirit as somber as a storm cloud," but her "genius as bright as lightning."

"Stanzas." February 2, 1856. The young poet is called a "star passing gloriously up the horizon of American literature."

"The World Is Lone Since Thou Art Gone." April 1, 1856.

"A Poet's Death-Day." May 9, 1856. Piatt is referring to Byron.

"The Last Soliloquy." May 22, 1856. Prentice calls his young correspondent's work "the noblest poetry ever written by a young girl," adding that her "name will be above the waves of time when she herself is beneath them."

"Early Friends." August 8, 1856.

"A Life-History." September 12, 1856.

"The Renunciation." December 13, 1856. Prentice adds "by one of the most glorious female poets the West has produced."

"I've Thought of Thee, Oh, Allan." February 16, 1857.

"Mattie's Grave." February 25, 1857.

"My Sister." March 28, 1857. By Sallie M. Bryan. Many of Piatt's early poems are autobiographical. Prentice likely knew her sister Ellen.

"A Reply--To Emma Alice Browne." April 17, 1857. Browne published several poems in the Louisville Journal, and this reply is to Browne's "To Sallie M. Bryan, My Idealia" that appeared April 14, 1857.

"Stanzas To _____, of Alabama." April 24, 1857.

"Last Night." May 13, 1857.

"My Star." May 28, 1857.

"Changed." June 18, 1857.

"Stanzas." July 1, 1857.

"That Picture." July 11, 1857.

"A Moon...Long Ago." (Title not clear.) August 1, 1857.

"When We Parted." September 4, 1857.

"Faithfulness." September 15, 1857.

"A Metaphoric Triple." January 13, 1858.

(On January 18, 1858, George Prentice published his "To Miss
 Sallie M. Bryan," which later appeared in his collected poems.)

"Only a Dream." February 12, 1858.

"A Tribute to the Dead." April 5, 1858. Subtitled to the memory of
 Dr. Warner C. Stevenson of Christianburg, Ky.

"Conrad and Medora." April 17, 1858.

"The Frozen-Hearted." April 30, 1858.

"I Met Thee in a Dream." May 17, 1858. Refers to someone named
 Clifford.

"Dying 'Mid the Roses." June 14, 1858.

"A Parting Tribute to the Graduates." July 1, 1858. Prentice
 explains that Piatt read this at her alma mater, Henry Female
 Seminary.

"Stanzas." July 5, 1858.

"Among the Shadows." August 2, 1858.

"That Song." August 19, 1858.

"I Dreamed That I Was Free." September 21, 1858.

"The Flowers You Gave." October 25, 1858.

"The Evening Star." October 30, 1858.

"I Met Thee First Neath Starlight Skies." November 25, 1858.

"Birthyear Musings." January 11, 1859.

"A Poet's Soliloquy." March 9, 1859.

"One Year Ago To-Night." May 18, 1859.

"Idols--A Dream." May 28, 1859.

"The Estranged." August 10, 1859.

"A Legend of the Lost Pleiad." September 20, 1859.

"The Parting." October 4, 1859.

"The Fated." October 24, 1859.

"A Rhyme of the Haunting." June 21, 1860. Has an epigraph from
    Shelley: "He is a presence to be felt and known/In darkness and in
    light."

"To Miss Lizzie C. Smith." July 18, 1860. A reply to Smith's poem
    "To Miss Sallie M. Bryan" in the same issue of the paper.

"Arthur Vale." August 7, 1860.

"Waiting--at the Party." September 22, 1860. Reprinted in The
    Capital.

(John James Piatt wrote a poem "To S.M.B." which appeared
    October 3, 1860. By this time their courtship fostered by Prentice
    was progressing.)

"An Eagle's Plume from Palestine." October 17, 1860. This poem appeared with John James Piatt's "Lines" and replied to his "Holy Land" imagery, but with her typical darker thrust. Published in The Nests at Washington and A Woman's Poems.

"My Dreams Were With Me." November 23, 1860. A somber poem about death that seems unusual at this time of her courtship.

"The Secret." January 18, 1861. Subtitled "A Fragment."

"To Night." March 12, 1861. Paired with "Moon-Rises," also perhaps by her.

"If Freedom's Miracle Should Fail." March 30, 1861.

* * *

Poems in The Capital: During the 1870s, many of SP's poems were published in The Capital, edited by Donn Piatt in Washington DC.

"The Uplifted Image." The Capital (March 26, 1871): 1.

"Paris (Jan. 1871)," "An After-Poem," "My Wedding Ring," and "A Walk to My Own Grave." The Capital (April 9, 1871): 1.

"Their Two Fortunes." The Capital (April 16, 1871): 1.

"Questions of the Hour." The Capital (April 30, 1871): 1.

"Shoulder-Rank." The Capital (May 28, 1871): 1. Published anonymously.

"My Ghost." The Capital (June 25, 1871): 1.

"To a Dead Bird." The Capital (July 2, 1871): 1.

"Home Again." The Capital (July 9, 1871): 1.

"A Woman's Answer (After Many Years)." The Capital (June 8, 1872): 1.

"Another War." The Capital (June 16, 1872): 1.

"Prevented Choice." The Capital (June 22, 1872): 1.

"The Funeral of a Doll." The Capital (June 29, 1872): 1.

"A Dead Book." The Capital (July 7, 1872): 1.

"Mock Diamonds." The Capital (July 14, 1872): 1.

"An East Indian Fairy Story." The Capital (July 21, 1872): 1.

"My Boys." The Capital (August 4, 1872): 1.

"The Sorrows of Charlotte." The Capital (August 11, 1872): 1.

"A Parting Gift of Youth." The Capital (September 29, 1872): 1.

"Her Rescue." The Capital (December 15, 1872): 1. Anonymous.

"The Grave at Frankfort." The Capital (December 29, 1872): 1.

"A Child's City." The Capital (January 5, 1873): 1.

"When the Full Moon's Light Is Burning." The Capital (June 8, 1873): 2. Reprinted as "When the Full Moon's Light" in The Capital (May 24, 1874): 2. Anthologized in The Union of American Poetry and Art (1880) as "Song."

"One Poet's Silence." The Capital (June 8, 1873): 3.

"A Ghost at the Opera." The Capital (June 15, 1873): 2.
Anonymous.

"Waiting - At the Party." The Capital (March 15, 1874): 6.
Reprinted from the Louisville Journal.

"If I Were a Queen." The Capital (April 19, 1874): 7.

"One of Two." The Capital (May 10, 1874): 3.

"Over in Kentucky." The Capital (May 10, 1874): 6. Reprinted
from Independent.

"Seeing Through Tears." The Capital (May 17, 1874): 2.

"Sometime," "A Masked Ball," Marble or Dust?" and "There Was a
Rose," with an announcement of A Voyage to the Fortunate Isles.
The Capital (May 24, 1874): 6.

"Worthless Treasure." The Capital (October 31, 1875): 6.

"Her Well-Known Story." The Capital (December 26, 1875): 2.

"Sad Wisdom--Four Years Old." The Capital (March 19, 1876): 2.
Reprinted from Appleton's Journal.

"If I Had Made the World." The Capital (November 5, 1876): 2.

"Calling the Dead." The Capital (December 17, 1876): 2. Reprinted
from Atlantic Monthly.

"Giving Up the World." The Capital (January 7, 1877): 6.
Reprinted from Atlantic Monthly and That New World.

"Faith in Fairy-Land." The Capital (1878).

Chronological Listing of Anthologies that Include Works by Sarah Piatt:

Poems of Place. Henry Wadsworth Longfellow, ed. 31 Volumes. Boston: Houghton, Osgood and Co., 1871. Contains "Kentucky," Vol. 30, pp. 25-26.

The Female Poets of America. Rufus Griswold, ed. Revised edition by R.H. Stoddard, Vol. III. New York: P.F. Collier, [1874]. 13 poems, pp. 443-446.

Songs of Three Centuries. John Greenleaf Whittier, ed. Boston: James A. Osgood, 1876. Contains "My Old Kentucky Nurse," pp. 303-304. Appeared as "The Black Princess" in A Voyage to the Fortunate Isles.

Masque of Poets. George Parsons Lathrop, ed. Boston: 1878. Contains "Her Word of Reproach," p. 77.

McGuffey's Fourth Reader. Revised edition. Cincinnati: Van Antwerp, Bragg & Co., 1879. American Book Company, 1896. Contains "My Ghost," pp. 178-180.

McGuffey's Fifth Eclectic Reader. Revised edition. Cincinnati: Van Antwerp, Bragg & Co., 1879. Contains "The Gift of Empty Hands," pp. 252-253.

The Union of American Poetry and Art. John James Piatt, ed. Cincinnati: W.E.   Dibble, Publisher, 1880. Contains "A Prettier Book," p. 445, "After Wings," p. 430, "Caprice at Home," p. 394, "Everything," p. 408, "Peace-Making," p. 375, "Sometime," p. 417, "Song," p. 397, "The Black Princess," p. 512, "The End of the Rainbow," p. 387, and "The Witch in the Glass," p. 521.

Golden Poems by British and American Authors. Francis F. Browne, ed. A.C. McClurg & Co., 1881. Reprinted in 1971 by Granger. Contains "My Babes in the Wood," pp. 30-31, and "Into the World and Out," pp. 286-287. By "Sallie M.B. Piatt."

The Cambridge Book of Poetry. C. F. Bates, ed. New York: Thomas Crowell, 1882. Reprinted by Granger in 1969. Contains eight poems by Piatt, pp. 419-421.

Among the Poets. A. A. Smith, ed. Philadelphia & Chicago: J. A. Ruth Co., 1883. Contains "My Neighbor's Confession," pp. 141-142.

Favorite Poems. Thomas Crowell, 1884. Contains "Questions of the Hour," pp. 436-437.

An American Anthology. Edmund C. Stedman, ed. Boston & New York: Houghton, Mifflin Co., 1900. Contains eleven poems, pp. 374-377.

The Hesperian Tree. John James Piatt, ed. Volume 1. Cincinnati: George C. Shaw, 1900. Contains seven poems and two prose works.

Songs of Nature. John Burroughs, ed. New York: Garden City, 1901. Contains "A Word with a Skylark," p. 157.

The Hesperian Tree. John James Piatt, ed. Volume 2. Columbus: S. F. Harriman, 1903. Contains eight poems and two prose works.

A Vers de Societe Anthology. Carolyn Wells, ed. New York: Charles Scribner's Sons, 1907. Contains "The Witch in the Glass," p. 156.

Poets of Ohio. Emerson Venable, ed. Cincinnati: Robert Clarke, 1909. Contains biography and 21 poems, pp. 183-201.

Little Classics for Oral English. S. S. Curry, ed. Boston: Expression Company, 1912. Contains "The Gift of Empty Hands," pp. 322-323.

The Home Book of Verse. Burton Egbert Stevenson, ed. First published in 1912. 8th printing, 1949. Contains "Into the World and Out," p. 27, and "After Wings," p. 119.

Kentucky In American Letters: 1784-1912. John Wilson Townsend, ed. 2 Volumes. Grand Rapids, Iowa: The Torch Press, 1913. Contains biography & three poems, I, 303-307.

The Little Book of American Verse. Jessie B. Rittenhouse, ed. Boston & New York: Houghton, Mifflin Co., 1915. Contains "After Wings," p. 169.

Joyce Kilmer's Anthology of Catholic Poets. New York: Halcyon House, 1940. Contains "A Word With a Skylark," p. 343. This anthology was first published by Boni & Liveright in 1917.

The LeGallienne Book of American Poetry. Richard LeGallienne, ed. New York: Garden City Publishing Co., Inc., 1925. Contains "The Witch in the Glass,"   p. 190.

Amphora. Thomas Bird Mosher, ed. Portland, ME: Mosher, 1926. Contains "Ah, Chasms and Cliffs of Snow," (By Sara [sic] M. B. Piatt), p. 14.

Famous Poems Explained. Waitman Barbe, ed. New York: Noble & Noble, [1926]. Contains "The Gift of Empty Hands."

The Nature Lover's Knapsack. Edwin Osgood Grover, ed. New York: Thomas Y. Crowell Company, 1927. Contains "A Word with a Skylark, p. 241.

The Bird-Lover's Anthology. Rittenhouse and Scollard. Boston: Houghton-Mifflin Co., 1930. Contains "A Word with a Skylark."

Patrician Rhymes. Rittenhouse and Scollard. Boston: Houghton-Mifflin Co., 1932. Contains "The Witch in the Glass."

Memorable Poetry. Sir Francis Meynell, ed. Franklin Watts, [1965?]. Contains "How Old Is God, Has He Gray Hair" ("Questions of the Hour").

Kentucky Authors: A History of Kentucky Literature. Sister Mary
Carmel Browning, ed. Evansville: Keller-Crescent Co., 1968.
Contains brief biography and three poems, pp. 108-111.

The World's Best Poetry. New York: Granger, 1982. Contains
"The Witch in the Glass," Vol. 1, p. 46, and "Term of Death," Vol.
3, p. 261.

American Poetry: The Nineteenth Century. John Hollander, ed.
New York: Literary Classics of the United States, Inc., 1993. 2
Volumes. Contains "Giving Back the Flower," Vol. 2, pp. 349-
350. Brief biography, p. 908.

She Wields a Pen: American Women Poets of the Nineteenth
Century. Janet Gray, ed. Iowa City: University of Iowa Press,
1997. Introduction and three poems,   pp. 180-185,

Nineteenth-Century American Women Writers. Karen Kilcup, ed.
Cambridge, MA: Blackwell Publishers, 1997. Introduction and 14
poems, pp. 284-294.

Nineteenth-Century American Women Poets. Paula Bernat Bennett,
ed. Blackwell Publishers, 1998. Contains critical biography and
24 poems, pp. 234-263.

Chronological Listing of Reviews of Sarah Piatt's Books:

Review of A Woman's Poems. By William Dean Howells. Atlantic
Monthly 27 (June 1871): 773-775.

Review of A Voyage to the Fortunate Isles. The Capital (July 5,
1874): 8. Reprints reviews from Boston Advertiser and Atlantic
Monthly, among others.

Review of A Voyage to the Fortunate Isles. Independent 26 (July 9,
1874): 11.

Review of <u>A Voyage to the Fortunate Isles</u>. <u>Scribner's Monthly</u> (August 1874): 501.

Review of <u>That New World and Other Poems</u>. <u>The Capital</u> (January 21, 1877): 6. Reprints review from the New York <u>Tribune</u>.

Review of <u>That New World and Other Poems</u>. <u>Appleton's</u> 2 (February 1877): 191.

Review of <u>That New World and Other Poems</u>. <u>Galaxy</u> 23 (February 1877): 286-288.

Review of <u>That New World and Other Poems</u>. <u>Scribner's Monthly</u> 14 (May 1877): 118-119.

Review of <u>Poems in Company with Children</u>. <u>Harper's Monthly</u> 56 (May 1878): 628.

Review of <u>Dramatic Persons and Moods with Other Poems</u>. <u>Harper's Monthly</u> 60 (February 1880): 470.

Review of <u>An Irish Garland</u>. <u>Scotsman</u>. December 26, 1884.

Review of <u>An Irish Garland</u>. <u>Academy</u>. March 21, 1885.

Review of <u>The Children Out-of-Doors</u>. <u>Atlantic Monthly</u>. April 1885.

Review of <u>An Irish Garland</u>. <u>The Pilot</u> (Boston). April 18, 1885.

Review of <u>An Irish Garland</u>. <u>Catholic World</u> 41 (April 1885): 138.

Review of <u>An Irish Garland</u> and <u>The Children Out-of-Doors</u>. <u>Graphic</u> 32 (July 11, 1885): 54.

Review of <u>An Irish Garland</u>. <u>The Saturday Review</u> (London). July 11, 1885.

Review of Selected Poems: A Voyage to the Fortunate Isles and Other Poems. The St. James Gazette. November 21, 1885.

Review of Selected Poems: A Voyage to the Fortunate Isles and Other Poems. Academy (London) 709 (December 5, 1885): 369.

Review of Selected Poems: A Voyage to the Fortunate Isles and Other Poems. Nation (Dublin). December 5, 1885.

Review of Selected Poems: A Voyage to the Fortunate Isles and Other Poems. Scotsman (January 1, 1886): n.p.

Review of Selected Poems: A Voyage to the Fortunate Isles and Other Poems. The Literary World. January 1, 1886.

Review of Selected Poems: A Voyage to the Fortunate Isles and Other Poems. Graphic. January 16, 1886.

Review of Selected Poems: A Voyage to the Fortunate Isles and Other Poems. The Freeman's Journal. February 19, 1886.

Review of Selected Poems: A Voyage to the Fortunate Isles and Other Poems. London Figaro. February 20, 1886.

Review of Selected Poems: A Voyage to the Fortunate Isles and Other Poems. The Saturday Review. March 13, 1886.

Review of Selected Poems: A Voyage to the Fortunate Isles and Other Poems. The Dial. Volume 6 (1886): 251.

Review of In Primrose Time. Atheneum 3069 (August 21, 1886): 237.

Review of In Primrose Time. Literary News 7 (August 1886): 239.

Review of In Primrose Time. Atlantic 59 (March 1887): 413.

Review of An Irish Wild-Flower. Atheneum 99 (January 2, 1892): 13-14.

Review of <u>An Enchanted Castle</u>. <u>Speaker</u> 8 (July 22, 1893): 81-82. Unsigned, but written by William Butler Yeats.

Review of <u>Poems</u>. <u>Literary World</u> 25 (September 8, 1894): 279-280.

Review of <u>Child's-World Ballads</u>. <u>Academy</u> 48 (1895): 381.

BIBLIOGRAPHY OF BIOGRAPHICAL AND CRITICAL REFERENCES TO SARAH PIATT

Appleton's Cyclopaedia. "Piatt, Sarah Morgan (Bryan)." Revised edition, 1900.

Austin, James C. Fields of the Atlantic Monthly: Letters to an Editor 1861-1870. San Marino, CA: The Huntington Library, 1953. Reference on page 58.

Bennett, Paula Bernat. "'The Descent of the Angel': Interrogating Domestic Ideology in American Women's Poetry, 1858-1890," American Literary History 7 (Winter 1995): 591-610.

Bennett, Paula Bernat. "John James and Sarah Morgan Bryan Piatt," The Garland Encyclopedia of American Nineteenth-Century Poetry. Eric Haralson, editor. Norwich, VT: Garland, forthcoming.

Bennett, Paula Bernat. Nineteenth-Century American Women Poets. Oxford: Blackwell Publishers, 1998. Critical commentary in introduction.

Bowerman, Sarah G. "Sarah Morgan Bryan Piatt," Dictionary of American Biography. Dumas Malone, ed. New York: Scribner's, 1934. See vol. 7, pp. 557-558.

Burress, Marjorie Byrnside. It Happened 'Round North Bend. Published by author, 1970. Reprinted 1987. See pp. 105-106.

Collins, Lewis. Historical Sketches of Kentucky. Maysville, KY and J. A. & U. P. James, Cincinnati, 1847. Updated and reprinted in 1968. Volume 1. Henry County. The Poets and Poetry of Kentucky. Contains biographical information and five poems, p. 615.

Coultrap-McQuin, Susan. Doing Literary Business: American Women Writers in the Nineteenth Century. Chapel Hill: University of North Carolina Press, 1990.

Coyle, William, editor. Ohio Authors and Their Books 1796-1950. Cleveland: World Press, 1962.

Davis, Gwenn and Beverly A. Joyce, compilers. Poetry by Women to 1900: A Bibliography of American and British Women Writers. Toronto: University of Toronto Press, 1991. Piatt not included.

Dobson, Joanne. Dickinson and the Strategies of Reticence: the Woman Writer in Nineteenth-Century America. Bloomington: Indiana University Press, 1989.

Dobson, Joanne. "Reclaiming Sentimental Literature," American Literature 69 (June 1997): 263-288.

Duychinck, Evert A. and George L., editors. "Piatt, Sarah Morgan (Bryan)," The Cyclopaedia of American Literature. 2nd edition, 1877.

Ellsworth, William W. The Golden Age of Authors. Boston: Houghton-Mifflin, 1919. Mentions periodical publication, pp. 45-46.

Farman, Ella. "Poet's Homes--No. VI: Mr. J.J. Piatt and Mrs. S.M.B. Piatt," Wide Awake (November 1876): 286-291.

Gray, Janet, editor. She Wields a Pen: American Women's Poetry of the Nineteenth-Century. Iowa City: University of Iowa Press, 1997.

Hanawalt, Jean Allen. A Biographical and Critical Study of John James and Sarah Morgan (Bryan) Piatt. Unpublished dissertation. University of Washington. Ph.D., 1981.

Hinkson, K. T. "Poets in Exile: Mr. and Mrs. Piatt at Queenstown," Critic 24 (February 24, 1894): 122.

Hollander, John, editor. American Poetry: The Nineteenth Century, 2 volumes. New York: Library of America, 1993.

Howe, Henry. Historical Collections of Ohio, 2 volumes. Cincinnati: Krehbiel & Co., 1902. Illustration, biography, and poem "When Saw We Thee?" Vol. II, pp. 365-366.

Howells, Mildred, ed. Life in Letters of William Dean Howells, 2 volumes. New York: Doubleday, Doran & Co., 1928. Letter to Piatt, Vol. II, p. 347.

James, Edward T. and Janet Wilson, editors. Notable American Women. Cambridge: Belknap Press, 1971.

Kilcup, Karen L., editor. Nineteenth-Century American Women Writers. Oxford: Blackwell Publishers, 1997. Critical commentary.

Kreymborg, Alfred. Our Singing Strength: A History of American Poetry. New York: Coward-McCann, 1929. Mention of Piatts, pp. 175-176.

Kunitz, Stanley and Howard Haycroft, editors. American Authors 1600-1900. New York: H.W. Wilson Co., 1938.

Mainiero, Lisa, editor. American Women Writers, 4 volumes. New York: Frederick Ungar, 1979, 1980, 1981. Article by Virginia R. Terris, vol. 3, pp. 387-389.

McHugh, Roger, editor. Letters of W.B. Yeats to Katharine Tynan. New York: McMullen Books, 1953.

Moulton, Louise Chandler. Papers. Washington, DC. Library of Congress.

The National Cyclopaedia of American Biography. New York: James White, 1898.

Pattee, Fred Lewis. The Feminine Fifties. New York and London: D. Appleton-Century Co., 1940.

Pattee, Fred Lewis. A History of American Literature Since 1870. New York: Century Co., 1915.

Petrino, Elizabeth A. Emily Dickinson and Her Contemporaries: Women's Verse in America 1820-1885. Hanover & London: University Press of New England, 1998. Valuable background, but no mention of Piatt.

Piatt, John James. Papers. Washington, DC. General Services Administration. U.S. State Dept., Record Group 59.

Piatt, John James. Papers. Washington, DC. National Archives and Records.

Piatt, J. J., editor. Poems of George Prentice. Cincinnati: Robert Clarke & Co., 1876. Introduction quotes several of Prentice's letters to Sarah.

Robertson, Eric. S. The Children of the Poets. New York & London: White and Allen, (1886).

Roller, Bert. Children in American Poetry 1610-1900. Nashville: George Peabody College for Teachers, 1930.

Scholnick, Robert J. Edmund Clarence Stedman. Boston: Twayne, 1977.

Stedman, E.C. Papers. New York City, NY. Columbia University Library.

Stedman, E.C. Papers. Durham, NC. Duke University Library.

Stedman, E.C. Papers. Columbus, OH. W.H. Venable (Box 7) and Dorothy Cameron Venable Collection. Ohio Historical Society.

Stoddard, Robert H. Poet's Homes. Boston: D. Lathrop & Co., 1879. Describes home in North Bend in 1876, along with biographical information and quotes poem "A President at Home."

Tardy, Mary. Living Female Writers of the South. Philadelphia: Claxton, Remsen, and Haffelfinger, 1872. Biographical information and three poems.

Taylor, Bayard. The Echo Club. Boston: James R. Osgood and Company, 1876. Mentions Piatt on pp. 136 and 146. Parody of John James on pp. 141-142.

Townsend, John Wilson, editor. Kentucky in American Letters, 2 volumes. Cedar Rapids, Iowa: The Torch Press, 1913. Biography in Vol. I, 303-307.

Tynan, Katharine. Twenty-Five Years: Reminiscences. London: Smith, Elder & Co., 1913. Personal description of Piatt along with a poem, pp. 311-317.

Venable, Emerson, editor. Poets of Ohio. Cincinnati: Robert Clarke, 1909. Biographical introduction and several poems.

Venable Papers. Dolores Cameron Venable Papers. Cincinnati Historical Society.

Wade, Alan, editor. The Letters of W.B. Yeats. New York, Macmillan, 1955.

Walker, Cheryl. American Women Poets of the Nineteenth Century. New Brunswick: Rutgers University Press, 1992. Piatt not included.

Walker, Cheryl. The Nightingale's Burden: Women Poets and American Culture before 1900. Bloomington: Indiana University Press, 1982. Period background; no mention of Piatt.

Watts, Emily Stipes. The Poetry of American Women from 1632 to 1943. Austin and London: University of Texas Press, 1978. Background; no mention of Piatt.

Whelpley Autograph Collection and Piatt Family Collection. Cincinnati, OH. Historical Society.

Willard, Frances E. and Mary A. Livermore. "Piatt, Sarah Morgan (Bryan)," A Woman of the Century. Buffalo: C.W. Moulton, 1893. 2nd ed., Detroit: Gale Research, 1967.

Worthington Papers. Columbus, Ohio. Ohio Historical Society.

INDEX OF TITLES

A Call on Sir Walter Raleigh 141
A Child's Cry 143
A Child's First Sight of Snow 56
A Child's Party 194
A Daffodil 211
A Dead Man's Friends 111
A Ghost at the Opera 127
A Hint of Homer 139
A Hundred Years Ago 180
A Lesson in a Picture 129
A Masked Ball 97
A Mistake in the Bird-Market 204
A Neighborhood Incident 146
A New Thanksgiving 210
A Pique at Parting 121
A Portrait at Youghal 152
A Prayer to Osiris 205
A President at Home 63
A Sea-Gull Wounded 176
A Shadowy Third 206
A Triumph of Travel 159
A Woman's Birthday 99
A Woman's "No" 207
A Word with a Skylark 167
After Her First Party 157
After the Quarrel 131
After Wings 46
All in the Bud and Bloom o' 209
  the Year
An After-Poem 64
An Irish Wild-Flower 165
Another War 184
Army of Occupation 65
Asking for Tears 108
At the Grave of a Suicide 163
Aunt Annie 89
Beatrice Cenci 78
Calling the Dead 109
Caprice at Home 125
Carrigaline Castle 169
Child's-Faith 136
Comfort through a Window 144
Confession 177
Counting the Graves 104
Crying for the Moon 88
Death before Death 50
Earth in Heaven 54
From an Ancient Mound 166
Gaslight and Starlight 39
Giving Back the Flower 178

Happiness--A Butterfly 203
Hearing the Battle-- 44
  July 21, 1861
Her Blindness in Grief 190
Her Cross and Mine 103
Her Last Gift 55
Her Word of Reproach 124
His Argument 168
His Mother's Way 148
"I Want It Yesterday" 73
"I Wish That I Could Go" 93
If I Were a Queen 67
In Clonmel Parish Churchyard 140
In the Round Tower at Cloyne 171
In Street and Garden, I. 150
Inspiration and Poem 202
Lady Franklin 102
Last of His Line 172
Leaving Love 82
Marble or Dust? 74
Mock Diamonds 186
"More About Fairies" 116
My Babes in the Woods 47
My Ghost 37
My Wedding Ring 41
No Help 107
Offers for the Child 52
One from the Dead 182
One Year Old 135
Over in Kentucky 79
Peace Making 112
Playing Beggars 61
Pro Patria 174
Questions of the Hour 57
Reproof to a Rose 120
Requiescat 162
Sad Wisdom--Four Years Old 106
Say the Sweet Words 81
Shapes of a Soul 49
Shoulder-Rank 181
"Some Sweetest Mouth 201
  on Earth..."
Sweetness of Bitterness 76
Talk about Ghosts 59
That New World 100
The Altar at Athens 101
The Baby's Brother 134
The Baby's Hand 115
The Black Princess 84
The Christening 151

The Coming-Back of the Dead   208
The Coming Out of Her Doll   161
The Descent of the Angel   123
The Fancy Ball   45
The Funeral of a Doll   86
The Grave at Frankfort   189
The Little Boy I Dreamed About   113
The Night-Moth's Comment   164
The Order for Her Portrait   72
The Palace-Burner   91
The Sad Story of a Little Girl   118
The Sermon of a Statue   156
The Sight of Trouble   137
The Sorrows of Charlotte   188
The Story of a Storm   160
The Thought of Astyanax Beside   145
   Iulus
The Witch in the Glass   155
Their Two Fortunes   71
There Was a Rose   66
This World   95
"To Be Dead"   133
To Frances Cleveland   199
To Marian Asleep   42
Tradition of Conquest   110
Two Innocents Abroad   153
We Two   105
Worthless Treasure   192